"This Day We Marched Again"

Also by Mark Christ

Rugged and Sublime: The Civil War in Arkansas (University of Arkansas Press, 1994), editor

Sentinels of History: Reflections on Arkansas Properties Listed on the National Register of Historic Places (University of Arkansas Press, 2000), co-editor with Cathryn Slater

"Getting Used to Being Shot At": The Spence Family Civil War Letters (University of Arkansas Press, 2002), editor.

"All Cut to Pieces and Gone to Hell": The Civil War, Race Relations, and the Battle of Poison Spring (August House/Butler Center, 2003), editor and contributor

"The Earth Reeled and Trees Trembled": Civil War Arkansas, 1863–1864 (Old State House Museum, 2007), editor and contributor

"Ready, Booted, and Spurred": Arkansas in the U.S.–Mexican War (Butler Center Books, 2009), co-editor with William Frazier

The Die Is Cast: Arkansas Goes to War, 1861 (Butler Center Books, 2010), editor

Civil War Arkansas, 1863: The Battle for a State (University of Oklahoma Press, 2010), author

I Do Wish This Cruel War Was Over: First-Person Accounts of Civil War Arkansas from the Arkansas Historical Quarterly (University of Arkansas Press, 2014), co-editor with Patrick G. Williams

"This Day We Marched Again"

A Union Soldier's Account of War in Arkansas and the Trans-Mississippi

The Civil War Diary of Jacob Haas
Edited by Mark K. Christ

The Butler Center for Arkansas Studies
Central Arkansas Library System
100 Rock Street
Little Rock, Arkansas 72201
www.butlercenter.org

First edition: March 2014

ISBN 978-1-935106-67-8
e-ISBN 978-1-935106-68-5

Project director: Rod Lorenzen
Copyeditor/proofreader: Ali Welky
Book and cover designer: H. K. Stewart

    Library of Congress Cataloging-in-Publication Data
Haas, Jacob, 1840-1906.
    "This day we marched again" : a Union soldier's account of war in Arkansas and the
trans-Mississippi / edited by Mark K. Christ. -- First edition.
      pages cm
    Includes bibliographical references and index.
    ISBN 978-1-935106-67-8 (pbk. : alk. paper) -- ISBN 978-1-935106-68-5 (e-book :
alk. paper) 1. Haas, Jacob, 1840-1906--Diaries. 2. United States. Army. Wisconsin
Infantry Regiment, 9th (1861-1866) 3. United States--History--Civil War, 1861-
1865--Personal narratives. 4. Wisconsin--History--Civil War, 1861-1865--Personal
narratives. 5. United States--History--Civil War, 1861-1865--Participation, German
American. 6. Wisconsin--History--Civil War, 1861-1865--Participation, German
American. 7. United States--History--Civil War, 1861-1865--Campaigns. 8.
German American soldiers--Wisconsin--Diaries. 9. Soldiers--Wisconsin--Diaries. I.
Christ, Mark K., editor. II. Hohenwald, Herman, translator. III. Title.

    E537.59th .H33 2014
    973.7'475--dc23

                              2014003180

Printed in the United States of America
This book is printed on archival-quality paper that meets requirements of the
American National Standard for Information Sciences, Permanence of Paper, Printed
Library Materials, ANSI Z39.48-1984.

The publishing division of the Butler Center for Arkansas Studies
was made possible by the generosity of Dora Johnson Ragsdale and
John G. Ragsdale Jr.

In honor of **Jacob Haas**
and the men of the Ninth Wisconsin Infantry Regiment.

In memory of **Betty Ann Billingsley**,
great-granddaughter of Jacob Haas,
whose family preserved Jacob's diary for 150 years,
and **Paul Emerson Wilson**, a history teacher,
who taught his son to truly appreciate the significance
of this unique historical record.

Table of Contents

Acknowledgements

Michael Wilson of Broomfield, Colorado, was incredibly generous in providing Jacob Haas's diary for transcription and annotation, and I cannot thank him adequately. Michael Edmonds of the Wisconsin Historical Society provided detailed links to specific materials on the Ninth Wisconsin available on the society's website, resources that were crucial to the project. Brian Robertson of the Butler Center for Arkansas Studies brought the Herrmann Schlueter diary to my attention as soon as he learned of the project; it was, thankfully, available on the Butler Center's *A Nation Divided: Arkansas and the Civil War* on-line collection. Kent Salomon provided a photo of his ancestor, Charles Salomon. My friend Tony Feaster created maps of Haas's travels, and my friend Tom DeBlack read and critiqued the manuscript, providing valuable insights and suggestions. Others assisted this project in ways big and small, and the fact that they are not mentioned here by name does not mean I am any less grateful for their aid.

Introduction

On September 17, 1861, twenty-two-year-old Jacob Haas enlisted in the Sheboygan Tigers, a company of German immigrants that would become Company A of the Ninth Wisconsin Infantry Regiment. Over the next three years, Haas and his comrades would march thousands of miles and see service in Arkansas, Kansas, Missouri, and the Indian Territory, including pitched battles at Newtonia, Missouri, and Jenkins' Ferry, Arkansas. During his service, Haas kept a series of diaries, which he transcribed into a single narrative in a notebook after the war. Sometime between 1920 and 1940, his son-in-law Herman Hohenwald translated the notebook from the original German, resulting in the "Diary of Jacob Haas As Soldier in the Civil War." Haas's transcribed notebook, as well as one of his original diaries from his war service and Hohenwald's translation, are all now in the possession of his great-great-great-grandson, Michael Wilson of Broomfield, Colorado.[1]

As was the case with many German Americans, Jacob was the son of immigrants. His father, Jakob Haas, was born on July 20, 1799, in Rettersburg, Rems-Murr-Kreis, Baden-Wuerttemberg, Germany. He married Katharina Krathwohl, born on November 4, 1803, in Necklinsburg in the same province, on November 29, 1826. The couple would have eight children, four of whom would not survive to adulthood. Their fifth child, Jacob, was born in 1840 in Wuerttemberg.[2]

---

1. Michael Wilson, emails to author, January 8 and August 12, 2012.
2. Jakob and Katharina Haas's children other than Jacob were Jacob Friedrich (born March 29, 1827; died at an unknown date), Katharina (born February 19, 1820; died March 8, 1830), Christian (born September 11, 1832; died March 24, 1833), Christian (born in 1836; died July 1, 1898, in Virginia), John G. (born September 27, 1843; died October 4, 1843), David (born about 1845), and Frederika (born about 1849). Jakob Haas reported $900 in real estate and $350 in personal property in the 1860 census. All genealogical information unless otherwise noted was found at ancestry.com or familysearch.com.

Jakob and Katharina Haas made the momentous decision to leave their politically and economically tumultuous homeland and immigrate to the United States with their four surviving children: Christian, Jacob, David, and Frederika. They chose Wisconsin as their new home, a territory that became a state in 1848 and was home to a sizeable German population. They may have been enticed by reports from settlers that Wisconsin was "a place especially suited for German settlement"; one writer, Dr. Carl De Haas (no apparent relation), wrote: "The region around Milwaukee made no particularly favorable impression on us; as soon as we got deeper into the country, however, the aspect of the land changed: swelling wheat-fields whose stalks could scarcely bear the heavily laden ears, corn-fields whose wide fanlike luxuriant stalks towered above our heads, alternated with the most splendid woods, which consisted mostly of thick-stemmed oaks. Herds of beautiful cattle covered the natural rich pastures, pretty log-cabins looked out from among trees and fruits everywhere and before them farmers were working with joyous faces and whole flocks of children, domestic animals, fowl, pigs, etc. could be seen." Such reports must have been tempting to a farmer like Jakob Haas. The family most likely came to the United States between 1850 and 1860, the first year they are reported in the U.S. census.[3]

Jakob and Katharina chose the village of Abbott in Sheboygan County on the shore of Lake Michigan as their new home. The Haas family was part of a massive influx of foreign immigrants into Wisconsin. According to the *Dictionary of Wisconsin History*, Wisconsin's population increased from 11,000 to more than 305,000 between 1836 and 1850. One-third of the new immigrants were foreign born, and only 48,000— most of them from Ireland—spoke English. The largest number by far came from Germany. A Depression-era study noted that "between 1850 and 1860 there was such increase in immigration from Germany that

3. Carl De Haas, *North America Wisconsin Hints for Immigrants* (Eberfeld and Iserlohn: Julius Badecker, 1848), 1, 23.

since the latter year the Germans have been the predominant element of foreign stock in the State."[4]

Many of the German immigrants had come to the United States after unsuccessful uprisings against the aristocracy in their native land, and many were strongly opposed to slavery in their new home. Some turned to the Democratic party politically, repelled by the anti-Catholicism of nativist Americans, but when the crucial election of 1860 was held, German-born Carl Schurz of Wisconsin campaigned heavily for Abraham Lincoln and the Republicans, urging the new citizens to support the new party. Other proponents of the Republican Party included Edward Salomon of Manitowoc, Wisconsin, who would become governor of the state in 1862 and lead Wisconsin through the difficulties of the Civil War. The German vote proved crucial to Lincoln in such states as Illinois and Indiana in his successful bid for the presidency.

After Confederate troops fired on Fort Sumter in Charleston Harbor on April 12, 1861, and President Lincoln called for volunteers to put down the Southern insurrection, Sheboygan County's men answered the call. One post-war account said, "Volunteers for the army came from every section of the county, strong in desire to show their loyalty to home and country, eager to wipe out the insult to the flag and willing to lay down their lives that free institutions should not perish and that the union of the states should not be disrupted. Lincoln's call to arms was answered by the German, the Scandinavian, the Irishman and the native born American without any distinction or hesitancy." The county would ultimately provide 2,215 soldiers to the Union cause, only 479 of whom were drafted—likely more than half of the county's population who were eligible for service.[5]

4. The village of Abbott was first settled in 1846 and established as a town in 1850. In a burst of post-war patriotic enthusiasm, the village name was changed to Sherman in 1865. Carl Ziller, ed., *History of Sheboygan County, Wisconsin: Past and Present*, vol. 1 (Chicago: S. J. Clarke Publishing Co., 1912), 259–60; "Immigration (19th-Century)," *Dictionary of Wisconsin History*, http://www.wisconsinhistory.org/dictionary/index.asp; Federal Writers' Project, *Wisconsin: A Guide to the Badger State* (New York: Duell, Sloan and Pearce, 1941), 48.

5. Ziller, *History of Sheboygan County*, 159–60.

Among the volunteers was Jacob Haas, who with the rest of his comrades in the Sheboygan Tigers would serve in the Ninth Wisconsin Infantry Regiment under Colonel Frederick Salomon, brother of the future governor. The Ninth would go first to Kansas, then march south in the first Federal invasion of the Indian Territory in a force led by Colonel William Weir of Kansas. Col. Weir's drunkenness and apparently aimless wandering through the Indian Territory during a brutally hot summer led Col. Salomon to arrest him in July 1862 and return the column to Kansas. A subsequent inquiry cleared Salomon of charges of mutiny. Salomon was promoted to brigadier general on July 18, 1862, and Governor Salomon appointed brother Charles to be the new colonel of the Ninth Wisconsin in September, a position he would hold for the duration of the conflict.[6]

The Ninth Wisconsin then embarked on a fruitless expedition into southwest Missouri in pursuit of Confederate forces, adding hundreds of miles to the thousands they would march during the Civil War. As part of General James G. Blunt's Army of the Frontier, the regiment would suffer severe casualties at Newtonia, Missouri, on September 29, 1862, before marching into Arkansas. The Ninth Wisconsin missed the heavy fighting at Prairie Grove on December 7, but took part in the lightning raid on Van Buren, Arkansas, at the end of the month, after which "the regiment was engaged in marching to various points, performing a kind of patrol duty" before going into winter quarters in February 1863. The men of the Ninth would continue their wandering through Missouri and northern Arkansas before being transferred to perform guard duty in St. Louis, ultimately shipping down the Mississippi to Helena, Arkansas, in October.[7]

6. E. B. Quiner, *The Military History of Wisconsin: A Record of the Civil and Military Patriotism of the State, in the War for the Union* (Chicago: Clark and Company, 1866), 541–42; Ezra J. Warner, *Generals in Blue: Lives of the Union Commanders* (Baton Rouge: Louisiana State University Press, 1999), 418; Quiner Scrapbooks: Correspondence of the Wisconsin Volunteers, 1861–1865, 3:6–7, Wisconsin State Historical Society, http://www.wisconsinhistory.org/civilwar/regiments (hereafter cited as Quiner Scrapbooks).

7. Quiner, *Military History of Wisconsin*, 532–34.

Around November 1, 1863, the Ninth Wisconsin marched to Little Rock, where they went into winter quarters and performed fatigue and guard duty. As enlistments expired in January 1864, 230 men signed up to remain in service, which earned Companies C and K furloughs to Wisconsin in February. In March, the Ninth Wisconsin marched south with General Frederick Steele's army in a doomed attempt to link up with a second Federal army in Louisiana and invade Texas. Jacob Haas and his comrades saw extensive combat during the month of April 1864, including heavy fighting at Jenkins' Ferry on April 30 in a desperate rear-guard action that saved Steele's army as it crossed the swollen Saline River in its retreat to Little Rock.[8]

The Ninth Wisconsin spent most of the remainder of the war in Little Rock. Non-veteran members were mustered out on November 17, 1864, and returned to Wisconsin. Four companies of veterans and recruits were consolidated into a battalion and would serve until mustering out in January 1866. The final statistics for the Ninth Wisconsin Infantry Regiment: "Original strength, 870. Gain—by recruits in 1863, 52, in 1864, 236, in 1865, 62; by substitutes, 16; by drafts, none; veteran reenlistments, 719; total, 1,422. Loss by death, 175, deserted, 25; transferred, 7; discharged, 191; mustered out, 739."[9]

Jacob Haas would precede his comrades in returning to Wisconsin, receiving a medical furlough in the summer of 1864, as he suffered from the effects of scurvy and three years of hard service in the field. He would go to work as a carpenter, settle in Lowell, Wisconsin, and marry Amalie Gohring in 1865. Amalie died at age 31 on February 21, 1873, from complications of childbirth; their infant daughter died one week later. He soon remarried, wedding Augusta Johanna Sette, the daughter of a prosperous farmer, on July 24, 1873. Jacob and Augusta settled down and raised a family, with Emma born in September 1874, Dora

8. Quiner, *Military History of Wisconsin*, 544–46.

9. Quiner, *Military History of Wisconsin*, 547. Dyer puts the regimental losses at 77 killed and mortally wounded, and 114 dead from disease, for a total of 191 casualties. Frederick H. Dyer, *A Compendium of the War of the Rebellion*, part 3 (Des Moines, IA: F. H. Dyer, 1908; facsimile reprint, Dayton, OH: Broadfoot Publishing Co., 1994), 1677.

in November 1876, Ella in February 1879, Clara in March 1880, and Frank in May 1883.[10]

The Haas family would move south, to Lafayette County, Missouri, sometime between 1873 and 1880, settling in the new town of Corder, a village that had been laid out in 1878 and incorporated in 1881. The move might have been in search of a more hospitable climate for the old soldier, who suffered greatly from his years of arduous service in inhospitable climates. Two old friends, testifying in support of Jacob's application for a pension in 1891, noted that "prior to his enlistment in the service of the United States in 1871, he was a sound and healthy man." By 1868, however, "said soldier looked pale and sickly and complained of Rheumatism, and from about his mouth, teeth, Ears and head." Other affidavits report that he was sometimes debilitated by his persistent rheumatism to the point that he could not work on construction jobs, and others would have to be hired in his place. Jacob Haas died on September 12, 1906, and is buried in Corder, Missouri.[11]

There has been little published on the Ninth Wisconsin Infantry Regiment. The most extensive account of the regiment's service is in *Michael Zimmer's Diary: Ein Deutsches Tagebuch aus dem Amerikanischen Burgerkrieg*, edited by Jurgen Macha and Andrea Wolf and published by Peter Lang in 2001. This volume includes the German-language transcription of a diary in the collection of the Wisconsin Historical Society, as well as an English translation. However, it is not annotated. Herbert P. Kakuske translated and published the 1895 memoir of his ancestor, Louis F. Kaskuske, in 1970 as *A Civil War Drama: The Adventures of a Union Soldier in Southern Imprisonment*, again without annotation. Most of the English-language information on the Ninth Wisconsin is in publications such as E. B. Quiner's *The Military History*

10. Mike Wilson, email to author, September 1, 2012. Augusta Johanna Sette was born on June 24, 1849, in Sundorf, Germany. She was the daughter of John and Dorathy Sette and lived with two brothers and three sisters in 1870. Her father reported $2,000 in real estate and $1,000 in personal property in the 1870 census.

11. William Young, *Young's History of Lafayette County, Missouri* (Indianapolis: B. F. Bowen and Co., 1910), 338; Pension materials from the collection of Michael Wilson, Broomfield, Colorado.

of Wisconsin: A Record of the Civil and Military Patriotism of the State, in the War for the Union, and William DeLoss Love's *Wisconsin in the War of the Rebellion; A History of All Regiments and Batteries*, both published in 1866. Other materials on the Ninth can be found at the Wisconsin Historical Society, though much of those are in German. A notable exception is Quiner's scrapbooks, in which he collected newspaper clippings pertaining to most if not all of Wisconsin's military forces in the war. The diary of Herrmann Schlueter, the Ninth Wisconsin's major, is held by the Butler Center for Arkansas Studies in Little Rock, Arkansas; in this case, the original is written in English.

Herman Hohenwald's translation of his father-in-law's memoir thus provides a rare glimpse into the experiences of a hard-marching and, when needed, hard-fighting regiment of German immigrants. Jacob Haas made note of the wild territory through which he marched, peppered by observations like this, as he walked through the flowering prairies of the Indian Territory: "It is beautiful, but even beauty, in the long run, becomes monotonous." He also candidly described the Ninth's habit of foraging liberally from the countryside and its denizens, tearing down fences for fires and bedding, and the ongoing fight against guerrillas; when a woman whose bushwhacking husband was killed came to camp to complain, she received this reply: "He wanted to have a lot of fun with the Yankees and blow out the lamp for as many as possible. Now his lamp was gone." While rich in battle action—particularly during the 1864 Camden Expedition—Haas's diary might be most useful to students of the Trans-Mississippi Theater for its detailed account of the exhausting efforts of Union soldiers to control one of the least-developed regions of the United States. Haas and his comrades rarely had access to railroads or steamboats. They walked from Kansas to the Indian Territory to Missouri to Arkansas in all extremes of heat and cold.

Finally, as an editorial note: In considering the Hohenwald transcription of Jacob Haas's original German manuscript, the decision was made to silently correct most spelling and punctuation errors—errors that most likely stemmed from the translator's relative skills with a type-writer—but to retain the spelling of proper nouns with the thought that those places and names reflected Haas's own interpretation of the English words.

Mark K. Christ
December 2013

Diary of Jacob Haas As Soldier in the Civil War.

Remarks

The following history and reminiscences out of my years of service in the Civil War, the Union army, are written with no purpose in view except that in later years I may have a clear conception of the things experienced in the best years of my youth as soldier in the Union army. The following pages convey the truth of my personal experience and are written only for my personal satisfaction, and that if occasion calls I may be in position to clearly remember the things experienced personally and with my comrades in the army and bear testimony to the truth.

J. Jacob Haas
Company A. 9th Regiment
Wisconsin Volunteer Infantry

Organization of the regiment.

The first call for volunteers for the creation of a regiment of young men of German descent was given in August 1861. The special inducement was that it should be under the command of General Siegel,[12]

12. Franz Sigel was born on November 18, 1824, in Baden, Germany. An 1843 graduate of the military academy at Karlsruhe, he immigrated to the United States after an unsuccessful 1848 insurrection. At the beginning of the Civil War, Sigel was director of schools in St. Louis, Missouri, a city with a sizeable population of German immigrants. He was made a brigadier general in the Union army on August 7, 1861, and promoted to major general on March 22, 1862. Sigel was a major force in recruiting German immigrants into the Federal army and served adequately in the Trans-Mississippi before transferring to the Eastern Theater, where his battlefield failures led to his removal from field command on May 4, 1865. He died in New York City on August 21, 1902. Ezra J. Warner, *Generals in Blue: Lives of the Union Commanders* (Baton Rouge: Louisiana State University Press, 1999), 447–48. Before his termination as head of the Union army's Western Department, Major General John Charles Fremont had promised Sigel that the Ninth Wisconsin Infantry would be assigned to his command, though this never happened. Stephen D. Engle, *Yankee Dutchman: The Life of Franz Sigel* (Fayetteville: University of Arkansas Press, 1993), 92.

who was known as a great commander and general and such we found him to be. This encouraged many, including me, to enlist. On Sept. 17th 1861, myself and many others joined the fast increasing Sheboygan Tiger Company.[13]

The company very soon had over 100 men and we were ordered to come to Milwauke, the headquarters of the regiment under General Siegel. We arrived at the Milwauke and camped in tents, 8 to 10 men in each. Soon the regiment was organized and the companies named alphabetically. The Sheboygan company, being the strongest, was called company A. Our time was mainly spent in drill and instructions.

On October 5th an officer arrived for inspection and part of the regiment was sworn in. I was out on guard duty and was not sworn in that day. On October 14th the same officer came back and others were sworn in. On October 18th he came again and this time I too was sworn in with others.

The regiment was now full and we had to remain in camp.[14] We had to drill every day until deep snow made it impossible. On October 26th the officer to swear in came the last time and swore in the last of the regiment.

Days went by drearily and some of the boys slipped by the guards and went into town. Some were caught but not much was done in the way of punishment except that they were put in the guardhouse. December and January came and we were still camping in cold and deep snow, on the shore of Lake Michigan, in Camp Siegel, in biting winds.

13. The companies initially recruited into the Ninth Wisconsin Infantry were the Sheboygan County Tigers, Burlington Guards, Wisconsin Light Guard, Madison Sharp Shooters, Sauk City Guard, Wisconsin Sigel Guard, and Manitowoc Salomon Guard. "The Ninth Regiment," Quiner Scrapbooks, 2:30.

14. The Ninth Wisconsin was camped in Camp Sigel, which was located north of Milwaukee on the shore of Lake Michigan. "The Ninth Regiment," Quiner Scrapbooks, 2:30.

Departure of the regiment.

On January 22nd 1862 we left Camp Siegel, Milwauke Wisconsin on train for Chicago and arrived at Chicago the same evening. We marched through town with military music to another railroad station.[15] Here we received coffee delivered in barrels. At 10:00 p.m. we boarded another train swiftly passing many small stations [and] hurried to Springfield, Iowa, and then going day and night on early morning of the 25th we reached Queme,[16] on the Mississippi. Here we left the train and were quartered in an abandoned theater, until daybreak. At 10:00 a.m. ours and company H with baggage and 50 wagons were ordered to Hannibal Mo., down the river about 25 miles. We arrived in the evening. With ferry we crossed the Mississippi and were quartered in a schoolhouse. Here the riverbanks are rocky high walls, often a small path only leading upward.[17]

15. Michael Zimmer of Company E, Ninth Wisconsin Infantry, wrote that "it was very moving when we marched through the town from one depot to the other. Everywhere they waved with cloths out of doors and windows, they applauded and cheered, the Chicago City Band welcomed us and led us to the depot." Jurgen Macha and Andrea Wolf, eds., *Michael Zimmer's Diary: Ein Deutsches Tagebuch aus dem Amerikanischen Burgerkrieg* (Frankfurt: Peter Lang, 2001), 122.

16. Quincy, Illinois. "A.B.C.," a correspondent from the Ninth Wisconsin, was quite taken with the town, writing, "Quincey...is a place uncomparable with others, partly surrounded by the Mississippi, which is ornamented with the quartering steamboats, the city itself resting on high hills, it gives it such a romantic appearance, that it seems like a queen sitting on her throne, ready to resist and never give up." Quiner Scrapbooks, 8:55. Quincy's *Herald* was equally impressed with the Ninth, with an editor writing, "For the time they have been in the service, they have evidently been well drilled, and their personal deportment while here was highly exemplary, not a single instance of drunkenness or other impropriety having occurred among them, so far as we have learned." Quiner Scrapbooks, 8:55.

17. Haas and the men of Companies A and H were lucky to be on detached service. Captain Herrmann Schlueter of Company E wrote of the experiences of the rest of the Ninth Wisconsin: "It was a miserable trip. Had nothing but a kind of cattle cars, almost no hay or straw between 50 +60 men in such a pen, and the thermometer 10-12 degrees below zero." Herrmann Schlueter Diary, Paul Dolle Civil War Collection. Found at *A Nation Divided: Arkansas in the Civil War*, Butler Center for Arkansas Studies, Central Arkansas Library System, http://ar-studies.contentdm.oclc.org/cdm/ref/collection/civilwar/id/145. Cited hereafter as Herrmann Schlueter Diary.

On the 26th we boarded a train on the St. Joseph Rail Way and went to Pamyra.[18] Here another regiment from Quincy was to meet us. Interference by rebels made them arrive late. At last they came and now together we were hurried on, past the soldiers' camps, protecting the railway.

Weston Mo. And Leavenworth.

Early on January 26th we arrived at Weston, Mo.—Here we were quartered in a Catholic Church. The town is almost abandoned by its people but full of soldiers.[19] It is situated on the bank of the Missourie River, which here makes the division line between Missouri and Kansas. On January 30th we marched across the Missouri River, on ice, seven miles and came to Fort Leavenworth,[20] in Kansas, but without stopping we marched on to the town of Leavenworth two miles farther west. Here a throng of people white, black, and red met us. All were anxious to see us and followed behind us until we were quartered in churches. Leavenworth is a fine town but scattered over much territory.[21] Here we had the best and laziest time. There is little snow. Steamboats are coming and going up and down the river. At this time the river is frozen over. Runaway slaves are coming in from Missouri.

18. Palmyra, Missouri.

19. Correspondent A.B.C. wrote, "Weston as I was informed by inhabitants there, was six month ago a lively business place, till the savage hand of secession reached it and destroyed its peace. Its population amounted to five thousand, now there are scarcely two thousand civilians there. All the house are inhabited by soldiers of the 12th Wisconsin and 18th Missouri Regiments." Quiner Scrapbooks, 8:55.

20. Colonel Henry H. Leavenworth established Cantonment Leavenworth with four companies of the Third Regiment of the U.S. Army in 1827 to protect travelers on the Santa Fe Trail. Congress designated Fort Leavenworth as the first territorial capital for Kansas, but Governor Andrew Horatio Reeder left it for more comfortable lodging at Shawnee Mission soon after his October 7, 1854, arrival. Fort Leavenworth was an important mustering and training base during the Civil War. The WPA Guide to 1930s Kansas (Lawrence: University Press of Kansas, 1984), 234, 240.

21. The Kansas territorial legislature passed an act on July 20, 1855, that made Leavenworth the first incorporated town in the territory. By 1861, it had a population of nearly 8,000 and held eight banks, five newspapers, and a variety of shops, manufacturing plants, and stores. WPA Guide to 1930s Kansas, 234–35.

Many Indians are here, men and women and children. They have their homes in the community.

The Great March to Fort Scott, Kansas.

The first march of our great journey to Fort Scott began.[22] With best wishes and deeds of kindness, led by music we marched out. At noon rain set in mingled with snow. It continued during the night. That night we spent under God's gray sky in water and snow. How glad we were when day came and we could march again. It was the only way to keep warm. March 2nd was somewhat gentler in weather condition, and so were the day from the third to the eighth. Every day we marched and mostly through prairie in the original wild condition. Grass is from six inches to four feet high but is now dry and brown. Wild geese, turkey and other fowl are in abundance. There were many rabbits and each boy in blue wanted to be the first to catch one. That gave much amusement.

Several times, when the wind was strong someone would throw fire into the dry grass and soon the prairie would be on fire for miles and miles around. People dwell only along the creeks and rivers and where these are lined with timber.

At last, on the eighth day of our march, we came to Fort Scott. Just when we went up the hill, into town, the wind blew so hard that we could hardly stand on our feet, and dust flew like smoke. It filled our eyes and noses. We could hardly see anything and hurried on as best we could without looking about. On the South side of town, on an open place, near a spring and creek we rested, and then made camp without delay, for a heavy thunderstorm came up. We had marched 140 miles.[23]

22. The U.S. Army established a base named for General Winfield Scott, located midway between Cantonments Leavenworth and Gibson, in 1842, garrisoning it until 1855. The army returned during the Civil War, fortifying the base, which became a major supply depot for Union forces in the Trans-Mississippi area. *WPA Guide to 1930s Kansas*, 193–94.

23. *The Military History of Wisconsin* states that the march to Fort Scott was 160 miles. E. B. Quiner, *The Military History of Wisconsin: A Record of the Civil and Military Patriotism of the State, in the War for the Union* (Chicago: Clark and Company, 1866), 541.

Fort Scott is a small town and is almost abandoned.[24] There are a few large Government buildings, otherwise no stores except a few Jews. People may think that it is strongly fortified because of the name but such is not the case.[25] One sees nothing but dilapidated buildings and fallen over walls on several hills on the West side of town. — In camp we pass our time in diverse ways. Toy windmills are now on almost every tent and such watermills along the creek. Playing ball and drill are daily diversions. Picket service is only around the camp and guards only around the prison camp. One day when I was writing a letter, I heard an unusual noise and yelling, jumped out of my tent and saw a number of the boys of the regiment in pursuit of a young buffalo which had strayed into camp. They threw rocks and sticks and would have liked to catch the animal but in anxious haste the buffalo clattered down the hill.

On May 5th several companies of our regiment and several companies of the Second Ohio cavalry[26] were ordered to Carthage Mo., and on the 7th our company and company F. were ordered to follow. Before we came to Lamar, much prairie had to be crossed. This little town in

24. "O.," a correspondent to the *State Journal*, wrote that Fort Scott "is a miserable place. The buildings which originally belonged to the Government, are substantial buildings, and cost from ten to fifteen thousand dollars each. During the Buchanan Administration, Government became suddenly convinced that is was no longer needed as a post, and sold the buildings and property at from one hundred and fifty to six hundred dollars each. Government now pays more per year rent than they were sold for." Quiner Scrapbooks, 8:57.

25. The base would later boast of breastworks, stockades, and three blockhouses called Forts Henning, Insley, and Blair. *WPA Guide to 1930s Kansas*, 194.

26. The Second Ohio Cavalry was organized between August and October 1861. Sent to scout the Missouri border in late January 1862, the regiment served in Arkansas, Kansas, Missouri, and the Indian Territory before returning to Ohio in December. The Second Ohio served the rest of the war in Kentucky and Virginia, returning to Missouri in May 1865. The regiment mustered out in St. Louis on October 12, 1865, having lost 83 men in combat and 184 to disease. Frederick H. Dyer, *A Compendium of the War of the Rebellion*, part 2 (Des Moines, IA: F. H. Dyer, 1908; facsimile reprint, Dayton, OH: Broadfoot Publishing Co., 1994), 1473–74. Luman Harris Tenney of the Second Ohio Cavalry wrote in his diary that the force left on May 6, consisting of Companies A, D, G, L, and M of the Second Ohio and "two Dutch companies." Luman Harris Tenney, *War Diary of Luman Harris Tenney: 1861–1865* (Cleveland, OH: Evangelical Publishing House, 1914), 13.

Mo. is on level country and has a Courthouse as its main building.[27] Here several soldiers had been killed by bushwhackers.[28] We marched on and reached Carthage on the 10th. It is a fine town and must have been a lively place commercially but at present it looks deserted and in ruins.[29] Here Siegel had a battle with the rebels.[30] There are many rebel bands around now but they do not attack us. O, here we get fried chicken, but we first have to catch them.

Many fine houses are empty. The people fearing us have fled. We were very hungry and entered homes. What a harvest! Mutton, veal, lard, apples, butter, ham etc. came from the cellar. O that tasted good. An old gray-bearded Sergeant thought he had molasses and delved in freely and then spit ferociously, for it was soft soap.

The rebels gone and the danger past we had to return. On the 13th we are at Lamar again and remain until the 15th. From Lamar we marched to Frey Wood Creek[31] and here we are camping over night. The next day we came back to Fort Scott and at our arrival at camp we were treated with fine hot coffee. We had marched 60 miles each way.

27. Lamar, the county seat of Barton County, was founded in 1856 and named for Mirabeau B. Lamar, who was president of the Republic of Texas from 1838 to 1841. *Missouri: The WPA Guide to the "Show Me" State* (St. Louis: Missouri Historical Society Press, 1998), 504.

28. The editor was unable to find any reference to this incident.

29. Carthage was platted in 1842 as the seat of Jasper County. The town was thriving at the start of the Civil War, but its fortunes changed following the battle of Carthage. The *Encyclopedia of the History of Missouri* states, "In October, 1863, the courthouse was burned, alleged to have been the act of Anderson's Confederate Company. At various times other buildings were destroyed, until the town was a complete ruin and the population was dispersed, few of the former residents returning when peace was restored." Howard L. Conard, ed., *Encyclopedia of the History of Missouri*, vol. 1 (New York: Southern History Company, 1901), 508, 514.

30. Franz Sigel led a force of around 1,100 Union troops against some 4,000 partially unarmed followers of Confederate Missouri governor Claiborne Jackson at Carthage on July 5, 1861. Sigel pressed Jackson's line until Rebel cavalry turned both of the Union flanks, at which time Sigel fell back under cover of his artillery. Sigel lost 13 killed and 31 wounded, while Jackson recorded 40 to 50 killed and 120 wounded. The action temporarily ended the Federal drive into southwest Missouri as Sigel's men retreated to Springfield. E. B. Long with Barbara Long, *The Civil War Day By Day: An Almanac 1861–1865* (New York: Da Capo Press, 1971), 91.

31. Tenney refers to this as East Drywood Creek. Tenney, *War Diary*, 15.

On May 16th we were ordered to go to Indian Territory and we started at once. The next day we arrived at the town of Humboldt. Here mostly German people lived — but the rebels had burned the best part of town. The houses standing were mere huts and most of these were empty. The Neosho, a strong river, flows by and is full of the finest fish and crawfish. Near the river, at a fine spring of fresh water, we made camp. The people brought cake, eggs, and butter of which we bought. They told us that the rebels had destroyed their homes and saw — and flour mill. The rebels had entered Kansas from the Indian Territory. The citizens had finely overcome and scattered them.[32] The country is rich in great deposits of coal. We are 45 miles from Fort Scott.

June 1, 1862.[33] We broke camp and on June 2nd came to a Catholic Mission for Indians.[34] In several large buildings, Indians received Instruction. At our arrival the redskins came from different directions to see the unusual sight. Men and women are almost entirely naked, nothing but apron on and that very small. Many of the children are en-

32. On September 8, 1861, Indian trader John Matthews led a force of Missourians and Indians on a raid into Humboldt, Kansas, where they "sacked the stores and dwellings, carrying off all the money and valuables they could find without resistance, all the men being absent." A quickly organized force of home guard cavalry pursued the raiders and killed Matthews in a skirmish. On October 14, a Colonel Talbott led around 300 Confederate cavalry into Humboldt, overrunning the home guard troops. Talbott "ordered his men to allow the women and children to remove their valuables and household goods from their dwellings, and even ordered them to assist." Most of the buildings in Humboldt were then set afire. L. Wallace Duncan and Charles F. Scott, ed. and comp., *History of Allen and Woodson Counties Kansas* (Iola, KS: Iola Register, 1901), 21–22; Albert Castel, *Civil War Kansas: Reaping the Whirlwind* (Lawrence: University Press of Kansas, 1997), 54, 63.

33. Colonel Charles Doubleday of the Second Ohio Cavalry led a force consisting of his regiment, the Ninth Wisconsin Infantry, part of the Tenth Kansas Infantry, and the Second Indiana Battery into the Indian Territory in pursuit of around 1,500 Confederate troops at Shoal Creek. *War of the Rebellion: A Compilation of the Official Records of the Union and Confederate Armies*. 70 vols. in 128 books and index. Washington DC: 1880–1891. Ser. 1, 13:408, in *The Civil War* CD-ROM (Carmel, IN: 1996) (hereafter referred to as *OR*; all references to Ser. 1 unless otherwise noted).

34. Osage Catholic Mission, now the town of St. Paul, Kansas, was established in 1847 and served both male and female students. Information found at http://www.osagemission.org/missionstory2.html.

tirely naked. The school children are fairly well dressed.[35] All, large and small, ran after the music. When the music ceased they wondered at the great shining pipes (Six large cannon) we had. These Indians were under Captain Rapp's second Indiana regulars command.[36] To satisfy these Indians one of the cannons was loaded and fired. At the roar of the Cannon many ran away and others closed their eyes and ears. Others laid hands over their mouths (Indian sign of fear). After several shots we went on through timber and over prairies, but mostly very beautiful country.[37]

June 3, 1862. Today we crossed a 26 mile stretch of beautiful prairie. Many-colored flowers cover the ground. It is beautiful but even beauty, in the long run, becomes monotonous. We saw timber and thought it 5 miles distant. We marched 5 miles and then the timber seemed but little nearer. Grass is high and many rattlesnakes and other very long snakes in it. On June 4th we came to Spring River. We waded through and on the other side came to a large camp. The many horses indicated that a regiment of cavalry was present. It was the second Ohio. Besides

35. Correspondent "Nine" wrote to the *State Journal*: "On the second day out we passed the Catholic Mission for the Osage Indians, a collection of some half-dozen large and well-built structures....There were large numbers of half-naked Indians riding about, each of them with a dog trotting behind them. Two separate yards were swarming with fat-cheeked, black-eyed, black-haired Indian children, who are put there for instruction. They are dressed in a civilized manner, and are curious without being either bold or impudent." Quiner Scrapbooks, 8:56.

36. Captain David G. Rabb led the Second Indiana Light Artillery Battery, which was organized at Indianapolis and mustered in on August 9, 1861. The battery would earn a fearsome reputation as it served most of the war in Kansas, Indian Territory, Missouri, and Arkansas before it was reorganized and moved to Tennessee in late 1864. The Second Indiana mustered out at Indianapolis on June 3, 1865, after losing 14 men killed and mortally wounded and 14 to disease. Dyer, *Compendium* 3:1111.

37. Nine wrote: "The Catholic Brethren, and also the Indians, were very much gratified at our presence, especially were the latter tickled with the idea of our 'shoots wagons,' as they termed Rabb's Battery, which was with us. To astonish them, the Captaid [sic] ordered some shells to be fired at a hill not far off, and after the firing was over the Indians rushed down there in a body to [find] them, but, having burst, the pieces escaped their attention. They were astonished that those big balls were not to be found." Quiner Scrapbooks, 8:56.

this the 10th Kansas Infantry[38] was on the field. They had arrived from Springfield Mo. and with them a large wagon train of provisions. They were awaiting our arrival. There is bush but prairie all around water is present. Small ovens of clay were now made and baking of bread begun. The first attempt was a miserable failure. The bread did not rise and was more like a stone than bread. It was distributed and then fried in pans, with lard. Biscuits were then made and with better success. The lard was derived from fried bacon.

June 6th 1862. Ours and three other companies of regiment, and the same were ordered out on a special expedition.[39] Artillery and cavalry followed. We made haste and soon came to the end of the great Cowskin Prairie, and here, from a hill, we saw in the bushes before us clouds of smoke arise. Quickly our guns were in hands and we made sure that the same were loaded. The cavalry, by this time, had caught several surprised rebels pickets.

Now we noticed a large river between us and the rebels, meandering through the woods. The river bottom was sandy and our wagons had great difficulty in crossing. The infantry waded through. Night had come over us but we pushed forward close to the camp of the enemy.

Soon bombs were thrown into the camp of the enemy and the Infantry made attack through the brush and timber. The cavalry attacked from the opposite side. But the rebels were gone. They had departed in

38. The Tenth Kansas Infantry Regiment was organized at Paola through the consolidation of the Third and Fourth Kansas Infantry on April 3, 1862. The Tenth fought in the Trans-Mississippi until late 1864 when it was moved east to serve in Kentucky, Tennessee, Mississippi, and Alabama. The regiment was discharged at Fort Leavenworth on September 20, 1865, having lost 28 men in combat and 118 to disease. Dyer, *Compendium* 3:1188.

39. Doubleday's expedition set out to attack Stand Watie's Confederate Cherokees and Missouri Confederates under Colonel John T. Coffey at their camps on Cowskin Prairie. They reached the camps around sundown on June 6. Coffey and Watie fled after the Second Indiana Battery fired six shots into the camp. No casualties were reported on either side in the brief engagement. Mark K. Christ, *Civil War Arkansas, 1863: The Battle for a State* (Norman: University of Oklahoma Press, 2010), 199. The four companies of the Ninth Wisconsin involved in the expedition were A, B, C, and H. Michael Zimmer recorded: "Each Company got four wagons so that everyone could ride." Macha and Wolf, *Michael Zimmer's Diary*, 128.

haste. Their tents, swords, guns, and pans with meat half fried all lay scattered on the ground. When we gathered again, we had about 30 prisoners white, black, and red.[40] The others, in the darkness, had made their escape. On an open space we now made camp. Next morning, close inspection showed different places where rebels had camped, but the campers were gone.

June 7th. Next morning we went back to camp "Spring River" and brought about 100 head of horses and mules we had captured in the expedition. Most of the animals were taken to Fort Scott because we had need of them.[41]

June 11th we left our camp, crossed the river and made camp on a large prairie near a fine Spring called Baxton Spring.[42] Here we had an easy time, built ovens, went swimming and picked maulberries. At one time 25 wagons were ordered to collect provisions. About 15 miles from camp we found a high hill, in open prairie. It was visible for a distance of 10 miles. This hill was flat at the top and about 50 feet square. It was a marvelous thing, in the open prairie. Soon we had filled our wagons and next day we were back in camp.

Coming back to camp to our great surprise we saw a large number of wild Indians with their small ponies and their tents pitched close to

40. The reference to black prisoners is most likely to slaves who were serving their masters in the Confederate army. The red prisoners underscore the deep divisions within the tribes in Indian Territory, many of which dated from the removal of the Cherokee, Choctaw, Chickasaw, Creek, and Seminole tribes from the southeastern United States in the 1830s.

41. Lieutenant David Carter of the Second Ohio Cavalry reported, "We captured about 75 prisoners and about 1,000 head of cattle and 200 head of horses"; Private Isaac Gause of the same regiment noted, "Lt. [Henry] Rush of our company was detailed to deliver the cattle to the beef contractor at Ft. Scott." Whit Edwards, "The Prairie was on Fire": Eyewitness Accounts of the Civil War in the Indian Territory (Oklahoma City: Oklahoma Historical Society, 2001), 17.

42. A. Baxter settled at Baxter Springs in 1850, establishing a sawmill and later a tavern along the military road between Forts Leavenworth and Gibson. Baxter Springs was the site of an October 6, 1863, incident in which Confederate guerrillas under William C. Quantrill attacked a small column including Major General James G. Blunt, his staff, and a regimental band. Blunt and a handful of soldiers escaped, while the guerrillas killed 87 soldiers. WPA Guide to 1930s Kansas, 441–42.

ours.[43] It was a colorful mixture of Indians, squaws and children from different tribes and names The wildest and most naked were called Osages. Some were Cherokees and these seemed more civilized. The former are copper colored and have their faces painted yellow, blue, black and green.

Indian War Dance

Here at Baxton Springs, we were requested to gather wood and brush to our camp and to be ready to make fire, when night would set in. The Indians would be ready to give a War Dance, around the fire. Everybody carried for we were all eager to see a War Dance.

When night came the fire was burning. Soon the sound of many small bells was heard in the distance. All eyes turned in the direction of the sound, but nothing could be seen. Suddenly they came, an orderly procession, grave in mien, up to the fire. The small bells were attached around their knees. They formed a circle around the fire. A few men stood out besides and beat time on a drumlike instrument accompanied with shrill whistling and thus introduced the dance. I am unable to describe the comic jumps and motions and at the same time each one shriek and yell how-e, how-e, ye, ye ,ye – how-el how-e ye- ye- ye etc. Their naked bodies were tinted with many different kinds of the loudest colors and many trinkets of the wildest sort around knees, necks and arms. Many had bunches of feathers white or colored upon their heads and long knives, arrows and bows in their hands. Some had tomahawks in one and a stick with a scalp on it in the other hand. Knives glittered, tomahawks were brandished. With wildest twisting of limb and bodies, one different than the other, with bloodchurning shrieks, beating of

43. Michael Zimmer's diary noted on June 11, 1862, that "during the night several Indians came who had been driven away by Indian Rebels and asked for help." Macha and Wolf, *Michael Zimmer's Diary*, 129. Wiley Britton wrote, "The refugee Indian families that had been in Southern Kansas since mid-winter came over and followed in the rear of the army after it entered the Indian Territory....They were mostly Creeks and Seminoles." Wiley Britton, *The Union Indian Brigade in the Civil War* (Kansas City, MO: Franklin Hudson, 1922), 62.

drum and jingling of bells, in the sheen of the fire colorfully painted and yelling like demons, they looked like a host of crazy devils from the lower regions of hell. After the dance they departed as they had come.[44]

Great Review.

Great review of all the forces was held by Colonel Weer.[45] Indians were included in the parade, but it was evident, they were not used to such events.[46] Unfortunately it rained, we were waters-soaked. Present were two regiments Indians, two regiments whites Infantry, one regiment cavalry and one Battery.

The March into Indian Territory

On June 28th all troops left this camp and marched into Indian Territory, until we came to a river. We waded through and made camp on a farm on the other side. It was called Hudson's Crossing, after the owner of the farm. The man had been plundered by a wagon expedition. There was little left in the way of provision. The next morning we marched on and soon came to the great Cowskin Prairie and on the other side of Grand River, where some time ago, at Round Grove, the rebels had been ousted.[47] On a hill, in thick brush, we made camp, with tents. At our arrival at this place we saw in the distance, on the prairie, a band of rebels on the march, but they soon disappeared. From the same direction, toward evening, came a regiment of Indians. They came and camped with us.

44. Michael Zimmer noted in his diary entry of June 27: "In the evening the Oswego Indians performed a battle dance. For this purpose they built a big fire around which they danced. It was awful to see how they brandish their tomahawks while they jump around the fire." Macha and Wolf, *Michael Zimmer's Diary*, 131.

45. William Weer, colonel of the Tenth Kansas Infantry Regiment, led the expedition into the Indian Territory. Wiley Britton wrote that Weer "had been up to entering the army, a lawyer of some ability in Wyandotte, and had a good military bearing, and would have been an efficient officer except that he was addicted to the liquor habit, which was frequently so pronounced as to unfit him for having command of troops in the field." Britton, *The Union Indian Brigade*, 62–63.

46. Herrmann Schlueter's diary noted "grand review [June] the 29th all Indians etc. turned out & in the evening we learn marching orders." Herrmann Schlueter Diary.

47. Haas is referring to the June 6, 1862, fight on Cowskin Prairie. See page 28.

Terror of the Night.

Sometime that night the entire camp went into uproar. In the camp of the Indians close by, one of them, to be sure of his horse, had tied the horse to his foot. He had done that before. For some reason when he slept, the horse became frightened and ran away, through the camp, across sleeping men dragging the Indian after. The cries of the terrified Indian and the other Indians yelling and running upset the entire camp. In the darkness no one really knew what was going on and all thought that the rebels made an attack. Fortunately no one fired a shot and no one was crippled by the run-away horse. In about ten minutes quiet again prevailed. What happened to the Indian and his horse I have never learned.[48]

We had much amusement with the Indians. We would split a stick, put in a coin and stick it into the ground. Indian children 5 or 6 years old would come with bow and arrow and from quite a distance, often with the first shot, shoot off the coin. Then the coin was theirs. The old Indians would watch with a great deal of pride and pleasure.

July 2nd. We continued our march and the next day we came to the camp of the Kansas troops, who had gone ahead of us. Most of them were in pursuit of a rebel band, whom they had surprised during the

48. Michael Zimmer wrote in his diary on June 29: "During the night there was an awful noise. Someone said the enemy was here, thus everyone pounced on his rifle half asleep, but some of us // were already here, so everyone fought over the rifles. It was so dark that no one could recognize the other, immediately we threw ourselves on the supposed enemy and tore the rifles from their hands and wanted to attack them with filed bayonet in order to sell their lives at highest price. Some grabbed their throats and held on to them absolutely determined not to let go. Finally the fight was solved and to our annoyance we found that we ourselves had been the supposed enemy. All this happened because two mules who had been tied together with a long piece of cable and who grazed near our camp. They had come too close to our rifles which had been put up in pyramids there. One had come from the right side, one from the left, the cable had caught them and tore them down. The cable had caught one of our comrades, too, and carried him away whereupon he raised hell, as he did not know what happened to him. The weather was very hot, 110 degrees in the shade." Macha and Wolf, *Michael Zimmer's Diary*, 132.

night. They had killed about 30 of the rebels. The rest had fled leaving provision train and equipment behind.[49] We camped here on the prairie but were about two miles from water.

July 4th We celebrated the day by thundering our cannons.[50] A volunteer regiment was sent out to look for possible signs of enemy but came back the next day.[51]

July 7th, we marched on over prairie, through timber and passed beautiful springs.[52] We saw many parrots babbling and flying about.

July 8th. We marched and camp was made in a bleak hill near woods. The heat was intense and springs were dry. Only one spring could be found for the entire army, but even this was all red and really unfit to drink. Even then too many thirsty crowded around and

49. Union scouts had determined that Colonel James Clarkson was camped at Locust Grove, while Stand Watie's troops were located on nearby Spavinaw Creek. Weer set out with about 6,000 men on June 28 and on the night of July 2 split his command to attack the two Rebel forces. They hit and routed both the next morning, with Weer reporting, "I completely surprised them, killed some 30, captured 100 prisoners [including Clarkson] and their entire baggage wagons, mules, guns, ammunition, tents., etc." Weer lost two men killed and four wounded. Christ, *Civil War Arkansas, 1863*, 200–201; Edwards, *The Prairie was on Fire*, 19. Michael Zimmer's July 2 diary entry noted: "the 2nd // Battalion of the 2nd Ohio Cavalry and the 1st Battalion of the 10th Kansas Cavalry [Infantry] Regiment were set out against a rebel gang and had a short battle with them. In it five of our men and 28 rebels died, and we took 143 prisoners, a good catch which pleased us all." Macha and Wolf, *Michael Zimmer's Diary*, 133.

50. A "Special Correspondent to the *Daily Wisconsin*" wrote to the newspaper: "The fourth of July was celebrated in as grand a style as resting, eating bean soup and boiled beef, firing cannon, playing of the regimental band and drinking the Sutler's whisky at $1 a quart could do it." Quiner Scrapbooks, 8:59. Luman Tenney of the Second Ohio Cavalry wrote of the celebration: "So many drunk. Officers gave freest license to the men. I was disgusted." Tenney, *War Diary*, 20.

51. Michael Zimmer of Company E, Ninth Wisconsin, wrote that the volunteer troop consisted of six men from each company, but because all of Company E wanted to volunteer, twelve men of that unit were selected. Macha and Wolf, *Michael Zimmer's Diary*, 133.

52. Michael Zimmer's July 7 entry said, "We did 16 miles, camped by a bad stony body of water where we found two wells, but they had very bad water." Macha and Wolf, *Michael Zimmer's Diary*, 134.

it was almost impossible to get to the water. Many were glad to suck wet sand.[53]

Next morning we marched on, but did not know whither. We marched, stopped—marched and stopped again and again. It was whispered that the entire Brigade was hunting water.[54]

But now soon better fortune was ours. We marched about a mile farther and stopped on a very dry prairie, near some timber. Here we found that we were at Spring River. The banks were very steep and rocky but eagerly we climbed down and swam and refreshed ourselves. But one of our men—Fred Rook[55]—drowned in the river. The drought became terrific and sickness appeared among men and horses. Great restlessness prevailed and all desired to march on. At this time differences set in between Colonel Weer and the Captain of the 10th Kansas.

53. Herrmann Schlueter wrote on July 8: "Col. Weir brought the command up to a sandy hill (no water within 3 miles from camp) and had the idea of digging Wells and then fortifying said Sand hill—beautiful prospect for the Summer Season. Boys called the camp—*Camp Desperation*. Men, horses and mules suffered greatly roads being dry & dusty and *no water* fit to drink. Thermometer 100 degrees (Farenheit)." Herrmann Schlueter Diary. Zimmer wrote on July 8: "After having done 15 miles we camped on a high mountain far away from the water so that we could not hear the frogs which croaked awfully. Water very bad, weather warm." Macha and Wolf, *Michael Zimmer's Diary*, 134.

54. "Alpha," a correspondent from the Ninth Wisconsin, wrote, "Water was so scarce that we were compelled to carry it several miles in a heat of 115 degrees, and then it was not of much avail, as it had to be gotten out of ditches and swamps. Putrid and dirty as it often was, we could make but very little use of it. Even coffee or tea we cooked could not be used." Quiner Scrapbooks, 8:60.

55. Tobias Martin of Company I, Ninth Wisconsin Infantry, drowned in the Grand River on July 10, 1862. Martin, of Town Lake, enlisted in the Ninth Wisconsin on September 5, 1861. According to a correspondent from the regiment, "Tobias Martin, belonging to Co. I, was seized with a fit of vertigo while standing in the water, washing some clothes, and drowned." There does not appear to have been any soldier named Fred Rook in the regiment. William DeLoss Love, *Wisconsin in the War of the Rebellion; A History of All Regiments and Batteries*, Part 2 (Chicago: Church and Goodman, 1866), 1071; Adjutant General's Office, *Roster of Wisconsin Volunteers, War of the Rebellion, 1861–1865*, vol. 1 (Madison: Democrat Printing Co., 1886), 630; Quiner Scrapbooks, 9:59. Michael Zimmer's July 10 entry said, "A Norwegian went to [spend] some time at the river, he played with a comrade and while his comrade wanted [him] to take off his clothes, he jumped entirely dressed into the water and fell backward almost immediately. Before some could help him, he drow[n]ed." Macha and Wolf, *Michael Zimmer's Diary*, 134–35.

Both had been made Brigadier General and the latter wanted to do something unwarranted and was arrested. General Solomon, our Captain, took over the command and soon we departed.[56] Here we saw some of the dangerous spiders called tarantulas.

July 15th. We marched back the way we had come and on the 21st we camped on a beautiful place, in shade and had relief from the terrible heat. But we had hardly settled to rest, when orders came and company A. and E. had to go out with an empty train.[57] We traveled the entire next day and the third day and mostly over larger and smaller prairies, beautiful but very sparsely settled. By the 23rd we had reached Hudsons Crossing and here we camped. Four days later our regiment arrived at this place with all the rest. Next day we proceeded nine miles farther and then again made camp. Here we found some beautiful springs.[58] From here we made several expeditions into Missouri to get feed for our horses. The place was called Camp Quapa, after the Indian of the same name.

56. The Union troops camped at Flat Rock on July 9. Herrmann Schlueter noted, "Camp very dirty. Weather hot. Thermometer one day 118 degrees in the shade" – and the troops languished there for days as Weer sat drinking in his tent. Supplies were so short that the men were put on half rations, and Weer refused to follow the urging of his officers to fall back and reestablish communications with Union forces in Kansas, leading Salomon to conclude that "his grossly intemperate habits, long continued, had produced idiocy or monomania." Finally, on the evening of July 18, Salomon sent his adjutant and 100 men to arrest Weer at bayonet point, and the next day the command began moving back toward Kansas. Salomon, reporting the incident to Brigadier General James Blunt, wrote: "I took the only step I believed available to save your troops. I arrested this man, have drawn charges against him, and now hold him subject to your orders." Blunt later investigated the incident and supported Salomon's actions. Herrmann Schlueter Diary; Christ, *Civil War Arkansas, 1863*, 203; Quiner Scrapbooks, 8:58–59.

57. Michael Zimmer noted that the train, which left at 5 p.m. after the worst of the heat of the day had passed, consisted of "a wagon onto which to load our rations and 17 wagons to drive with....We did another 22 miles and camped in the morning at 2 o'clock on a breezy hill. Weather 117 degrees." Macha and Wolf, *Michael Zimmer's Diary*, 136–37.

58. Herrmann Schlueter wrote on July 26: "Regt. with exception of some companies marched to Quaw Paw Nation—fine water (we know how to appreciate it)." Michael Zimmer noted, "Companies E, K and G...had to stay to guard headquarters." Herrmann Schlueter Diary; Macha and Wolf, *Michael Zimmer's Diary*, 137.

August 6th. We moved forward and came to Baton Springs. We did not stop but kept on marching for four days, in heat and dust. It was a strenuous march. One prairie was 30 miles long and we made it mostly by night. On August 11th we came back to Fort Scott. We found the town and conditions much improved and prospering. The entire expedition was 542 miles mostly in and out of Indian territory. We came within 12 miles of Fort Gibson, Arkansas [Indian Territory].[59]

Wagon Expedition to Missouri.

On August 12th the 9th Wisconsin and the 10th Kansas regiments were ordered to be ready to march, with provisions for 5 days, because it would be a larger expedition. In the evening we departed. About 80 wagons were in the train. First we made several fake moves then set out a long train. Without stopping we traveled three nights and two days and saw beautiful country and orchards. We came through villages where much vandalism had been done.

On August 27th[60] we were 5 miles from Lone Jack.[61] Here we intended to rest and eat meat. We butchered largely and being very hungry we roasted some, on sticks on the open fire, and other was put in kettles with beans. When all was about half done alarm was given and order to march. Quickly we gulped down a few bites and destroyed the rest. Soon we stood in line for our company. We were ordered backward, for the rebels aware of our nearness wanted to escape. But hardly had

---

59. Fort Gibson was actually in the Indian Territory, overlooking the Grand River's junction with the Arkansas River. Christ, *Civil War Arkansas, 1863*, 5–6.

60. Actually, it was August 17.

61. Lone Jack, platted in 1841, was named for its landmark: a solitary blackjack oak tree. Bill Earngey, *Missouri Roadsides: The Traveler's Companion* (Columbia: University of Missouri Press, 1995), 162–63. Confederate forces attacked Unionist militiamen in Lone Jack on August 11, 1862, in a six-hour battle that one writer characterized thusly: "Nearly all the Civil War fighting in Jackson County was marked by vindictiveness, but at Lone Jack the feeling between Unionists and Confederates was unusually intense." Both sides lost around 125 killed and wounded in the fighting. Conard, *Encyclopedia of the History of Missouri*, vol. 4, 108.

we made a mile when heavy rains encircled us. We had to stop where we were along the fences on the road.[62]

Next morning pursuit was taken up again and continued for three days, in greatest haste. The rear of the enemy we pressed hard and killed many. The rest fled as fast as they could from the state of Missouri. We followed them to Monte Cello,[63] where we were in a heavy thunderstorm, practically all night. In the morning we went to a cornfield to satisfy our hunger. Besides the corn we had fresh meat.[64] After this we entered our wagons and started homeward. The second day August 22nd—we came back to Fort Scott Kansas. During this expedition many lost their hats. The men went to sleep and the hats rolled off the wagons. The fine orchards along the way lost quite a bit of their fruit. During the 10 days with wagons and mules, we had made 452 miles.

Wagon Expedition No. 2 To Missouri.

After we had been in camp for several days again we received orders to go to Missouri. We started in direction of our former trip but advanced to Monte Cello only. We found no trace of the enemy and on Sept. 1st returned to Fort Scott. We had made 148 miles.[65]

---

62. Herrmann Schlueter wrote: "At Lone Jack we made preparations to bivouac there, but soon we were put to march back again, night came and it began to rain, after we marched about one mile it became so dark that it was impossible to march any further, so we had to remain where we stood in the muddy road—and so we stood there till the next morning—immovable." Michael Zimmer concluded: "This was a sad night." Herrmann Schlueter Diary; Macha and Wolf, *Michael Zimmer's Diary*, 142.

63. Monticello, founded in 1829 in an area troubled by malaria, was eclipsed by Glasgow as a retail and shipping center after the war. Earngey, *Missouri Roadsides*, 101–2.

64. Michael Zimmer's diary entry for August 21 said, "Scarcely had we laid down, when it started to rain heavily. Our stock of crackers was exhausted. We only had meat which we prepared the way Indians prepare it." Herrmann Schlueter enjoyed the repast, writing, "Killed some Beef and Hogs and had a splendid Breakfast (Indian Fashion)." Macha and Wolf, *Michael Zimmer's Diary*, 142; Herrmann Schlueter Diary.

65. Herrmann Schlueter wrote: "On the 29th we made a similar trip to Montevallo Nevada and vicinity, returned Monday Sept. 1st," while Michael Zimmer observed, "We returned to Fort Scott in the evening without having accomplished anything." Herrmann Schlueter Diary; Macha and Wolf, *Michael Zimmer's Diary*, 143.

The March to Missouri.

After several days new preparations for the expedition were made. On Sept. 13th we left Fort Scott and marched to Ivy Wood Creek,[66] where we made camp. Next morning we proceeded to Lamar. Again we continued and on the 18th came through Greenfield. A small but very fine and rich town.[67] High hills are on one side of the town and on one of them we camped for the night. Water we had to get a distance of two miles. Nevertheless coffee was wanted. Next day we marched 24 miles, all through timber and then made camp again on a hill with a river before us. Next morning we swerved to the right and proceeded in another direction. On the 22nd we came to Sarconie, situated in a deep valley and surrounded by high, steep, wooded hills. Once there had been good trade and stored but now all was empty.[68] Before a large beautiful home we halted. Other companies were outside of the town, on a high hill.

Sept 29th. Four companies of our regiment with two cannon and cavalry from the 9th Kansas[69] were sent out for intelligence and location and strength of the enemy.[70] One of our artillerists went to get feed for his horse. When about ready to lift his load two rebels jumped upon him, pointed their guns and told him to hand over his

66. Schlueter wrote that this was Drywood Creek. Herrmann Schlueter Diary.

67. Greenfield was platted in 1841 as the county seat of Dade County and was harassed frequently by Confederate raiders after Union garrisons were established there later in the war. Earngey, *Missouri Roadsides*, 106.

68. Michael Zimmer wrote: "We found a village with the strange name of Sarcoxie, Missouri. There are many stores, a sawmill, a wool-factory, and a mill with a work crew." Macha and Wolf, *Michael Zimmer's Diary*, 145. Sarcoxie was founded in 1831 as Centerville, but its name was changed to that of a Delaware Indian chief after it was learned that there already was a Centerville, Missouri. Earngey, *Missouri Roadsides*, 40.

69. The Ninth Kansas Cavalry was organized at Fort Leavenworth on March 27, 1862, by consolidating independent companies and squadrons formed for other regiments. The regiment saw all of its service in the Trans-Mississippi and lost 53 men killed or mortally wounded and 142 to disease. Dyer, *Compendium*, 2:1183–84.

70. The detachment consisted of "four companies of the Ninth Wisconsin Infantry, two companies of the Sixth Kansas Cavalry under Captain David Mefford, about fifty men of the Third Indian Regiment, and a section of Captain J. Stockton's Battery." Britton, *Union Indian Brigade*, 92.

two revolvers. They added that death was certain for him. The artillerist kept cool, reached for his two guns already cocked, one in each hand, and down came the two rebels. He now took their guns and brought them to the commander Solomon. The commander had the two dead rebels brought in and one of the guns was presented to the artillerist.[71] Soon after, a young woman, crying bitterly, came to the commander complaining that her husband had been killed, but stating that she had warned him and begged him not to go because she had a premonition that he would not return. But he wanted to have a lot of fun with the Yankees and blow out the lamp for as many as possible. Now his lamp was gone.

At the time our intelligence expedition had been sent out the rebels had concentrated at a small town "Newton"[72] and had thrown up a wall and fortified themselves. On three sides they had prairie. It was about 16 miles from our camp—Sarconie. On Sept 30th our party encountered the rebel pickets and drove them before them close to the town and fortification. An attack was made and the rebels driven into their walls. Here the rebels were well protected.[73] Our force was eager to at-

71. Michael Zimmer recounted this incident, writing that a trooper from the Second Ohio Cavalry and an artilleryman from the Third Kansas Battery "had lagged behind to get some water melons, when they had them, the artilleryman sat down to taste his melons, but was // disturbed in a very unfriendly way. When he looked up, two highwaymen stood in front of him and demanded his weapons and wanted to take him prisoner. He said, I can't do anything against two, drew his revolver, as he did this, he cocked the gun and shot the first through the breast. The other shot him, but the gun didn't go off, whereupon he turned and ran away, but three bullets caught up with him, the third shot him down. Then our hero hurried to reach the regiment and announced it. Immediately an ambulance was sent to get them. They were both declared dead. Both revolvers and one of the horses were given to our hero by General Solomon." Macha and Wolf, *Michael Zimmer's Diary*, 145–46.

72. Though the area was settled in the early 1830s, the town of Newtonia was not established until 1857 and was mostly destroyed during the Civil War. Earngey, *Missouri Roadsides*, 192. When the Civil War started, 97 people lived in Newtonia. Larry Wood, *The Two Civil War Battles of Newtonia* (Charleston, SC: The History Press, 2010), 15.

73. The Confederate force at Newtonia consisted of about 4,000 cavalry under the command of Colonel Douglas H. Cooper. Michael E. Banasik, *Reluctant Cannoneer: The Diary of Robert T. McMahan of the Twenty-fifth Independent Ohio Light Artillery* (Iowa City, IA: Press of the Camp Pope Bookshop, 2000), 62n.

tack the cavalry ahead. When they were close to the wall the enemy fired. Our cavalry fled in panic and crashed through the Infantry behind them. Now the rebels attacked but our infantry scattered them, took many prisoners and many were killed. Others escaped and came back to us. Our artillery was hidden in the woods. We heard the roar of the cannon but had no information, did not know their position and therefore could not go to their rescue. We stood ready on the prairie. At last, when dispatch came we hurried there but it was too late.[74]

We took position on a hill opposite the town and bombarded with six guns. The rebels answered with gun fire but wounded only one man. Toward evening we retired into the woods. Now the rebels came out. We took them under fire and soon they returned into their walls. We returned to the prairie at Sarconie and camped, in heavy rain, without tents.[75]

74. On September 29, 1862, Lieutenant Colonel Arthur Jacobi led companies D, G, E, and H of the Ninth Wisconsin Infantry, a section of Captain J. B. Stockton's Ohio Battery, and a squadron of the Ninth Kansas Cavalry on a reconnaissance to Newtonia, where Confederate troops were believed to be gathering. The Union force drove the Rebel pickets behind a stone wall, and Jacobi ordered a bayonet charge, during which the Wisconsin troops realized the Confederates numbered in the thousands instead of the hundreds. A correspondent from the Ninth wrote that the Kansas cavalrymen fled the field and, "Our four companies...fought with the courage of lions, [fought] their way through the enemy, and thus saved their pieces of artillery, which they did not want to lose for no price." Falling back into a wooded area, the German soldiers were surrounded and, another correspondent wrote, "it was a mutual and savage butchery, but the superiority of the enemy crushed our brave soldiers after a short time." Union casualties totaled 28 killed and 167 taken prisoner, including 51 wounded. Only about 30 Ninth Wisconsin men escaped the battlefield. Quiner Scrapbooks, 8:62; Quiner, *Military History of Wisconsin*, 542. Michael Zimmer was one of only seven men from Company E who escaped being captured. He wrote that he and Hermann Kruener returned to the battlefield after Union reinforcements arrived: "When we had marched about a quarter of a mile, we had found several dead comrades who lay entirely naked on the side of the road. Just a short distance away we found several dead who were awfully mutilated and disgracefully injured. Oh, it was terrible to see them, as their clothes had been taken off. We found a dead body, too, that had half been eaten by pigs. We searched the whole battlefield for wounded comrades whom we might have helped, but everyone we found was dead." Macha and Wolf, *Michael Zimmer's Diary*, 148–49.

75. Salomon ordered the Sixth Kansas Volunteer Cavalry, Third Indian Home Guard, Allen's battery, Stockton's battery, the Tenth Kansas Infantry, and Ninth Wisconsin Infantry to Newtonia. The Union force contained the Confederates within their defenses, then fell back to Sarcoxie that evening. *OR*, 13:288.

A New Attack.

On Oct. 4th early in the morning our entire forces proceeded against Newton to make a united attack against the rebel stronghold. It was known that strong re-enforcements were on the way from Springfield, under General Schoffield[76] and were to attack the rebels from the opposite side.—At daybreak the rebel pickets were driven back and soon we faced the rebel nest. Our cannon roared into Newton but there was no answer. We were in battle array; the Indians gave the war cry, on the other side of town black regiments—our re-enforcements—advanced. But the rebels had escaped, leaving one cannon behind. One rebel reporter was captured at the writing desk. He had no information of our presence and first thought we were rebels.[77]

To March From Newton To Pea Ridge.

We left Newton on Oct. 5th marched 10 miles and then made camp on a farm in dense brush near a creek called Camp Indian Creek. Here we rested several days and were paid.[78] On Oct. 14th we came to

76. John M. Schofield was born on September 29, 1831, at Gerry in western New York. An 1853 graduate of West Point, he served as Nathaniel Lyon's chief of staff during the Wilson's Creek campaign. He was promoted to brigadier general on November 21, 1861, and given command of all Union militia in Missouri. Schofield commanded the Army of the Frontier from October 1862 to April 1863 and was confirmed as a major general on May 12, 1863. He later achieved division and corps command east of the Mississippi River and commanded the troops that crippled John Bell Hood's Army of Tennessee at Franklin in November 1864. Schofield would retire as a lieutenant general and was buried at Arlington National Cemetery after his March 4, 1906, death. Warner, *Generals in Blue*, 425–26.

77. Brigadier General John M. Schofield arrived at Sarcoxie on October 3, and the next morning approached Newtonia with the divisions of Blunt and Totten, about 12,000 men. Schofield reported: "The enemy's force was not concentrated and he offered but feeble resistance. A running artillery fight of about two hours' duration was the only engagement that could be brought on. Only trifling loss on either side." *OR*, 13:311. While the fight at Newtonia was a relatively minor affair, it and its aftermath resulted in every organized Confederate force in Missouri being driven from the state. Clement A. Evans, ed., *Confederate Military History* Extended Edition, Vol. XII Missouri (Confederate Publishing Co., 1899; reprint with new material, Wilmington, NC: Broadfoot Publishing Co., 1988), 102.

78. Herrmann Schlueter wrote that the regiment stayed at Indian Creek from October 5 to October 10. Herrmann Schlueter Diary.

Virgins Spring, so called because of a large flowing spring.[79] Here is a
fine farm and a large orchard. The fine fruit. The fine fruit disappeared
in a short time.

From here we proceeded to Hittsville, a small town.[80] Here we found
the Springfield forces moving through with a long train.[81] We marched
after them on the same road. Toward the morning we had climbed a
high, steep hill, were very tired and rested a little. At daybreak we came
to Elkhorn Tavern—a large tavern once but no more.[82] We now were
close to Pea Ridge battle field, where general Siegel became a hero and
vanquished the rebels. Here a barrel was set into fire and breakfast was
prepared best we could. Hard herbs were mashed and cooked in tin cans
until a little soft. Then we went on about two miles farther and came to
the real Pea Ridge Battle Field. Here we camped on a cleared place, near
a house under dry fruit trees. It had been a former campground of the
rebels. Some of their camp material had been left, for they had departed
in a hurry just before our arrival. A division of our cavalry was sent in
pursuit and captured several Howitzers and killed some of the enemy.[83]
At the house we camped were several beautiful springs. We are 8 miles
into the state of Arkansas. Shells and parts of shells and trees torn by
shells tell the tale of the severity of the battle here fought.

79. Schlueter noted this location as the head of School Creek, and that the camp
was called "Camp Curtis." Herrmann Schlueter Diary.

80. Actually Keetsville. Michael Zimmer wrote: "We found a village called
Keezville which was entirely destroyed." Macha and Wolf, *Michael Zimmer's Diary*, 152.

81. These troops were the Missouri Division led by Brigadier General Francis
Herron. They, with the divisions of Blunt and Totten, made up the newly created Army
of the Frontier, commanded by Schofield. William L. Shea, *Fields of Blood: The Prairie
Grove Campaign* (Chapel Hill: University of North Carolina Press, 2009), 29.

82. An Iowa trooper wrote of Elkhorn Tavern: "The old tavern itself is a dreary
picture enough. A cannon ball or two made several breaches in the logs, and numerous
rifle balls imbedded in it gave evidence of the struggle that raged around it." Shea,
Fields of Blood, 30.

83. Blunt led most of his division toward the Indian Territory on October 20, 1862,
intent on attacking Brigadier General Douglas H. Cooper's Confederates. On the morning of October 22, he hit them at Old Fort Wayne and, though outnumbered, routed
the Rebel troops, capturing a battery of artillery among other supplies. Blunt lost five
dead and five wounded, while Cooper lost at least three dead, 25 wounded, and 35
missing. Shea, *Fields of Blood*, 35–42.

October 24th and 25th. During the night heavy snow fell and it was really cold but warmer weather followed quickly. On October 28th we left Pea Ridge and soon came to Bentonville a once beautiful but now entirely ruined town. The reason for the destruction is this: when General Siegel camped at this town many of his soldiers were given poisoned water. In retaliation the general set fire to many of the best homes. Ruins only remained.[84]

October 25th

This day we marched again. Fine apple orchards are around but they have suffered by frost. Rocky hills and deep valleys make beautiful panorama. Our company A. was in the advance. Soon Intelligence came that our cavalry, in the lead, had been fired on from a Mill. The perpetrators escaped, but the mill was stormed and burned.[85] We marched on and came to Maysville, a very insignificant little nest, on the edge of a prairie, not far from Fort Wayne.[86] We made camp under large Walnut trees near the place our cavalry had captured several guns from the rebels. Next day we returned to the old burned mill. Here we camped and had bi-monthly inspection.

84. On February 18, 1862, a Union strike force of cavalry and artillery led by Brigadier General Alexander Asboth hit Bentonville, capturing several Confederate soldiers and some supplies. After administering the oath of allegiance to the town's residents, the Federals left, but one trooper returned to fill his canteen with whiskey. A Confederate soldier killed him, and the people of Bentonville hid his body in an outhouse. A Union search party found the body and burned much of the town in retaliation. Mark K. Christ, "Action at Bentonville," *Encyclopedia of Arkansas History & Culture*, http://www.encyclopediaofarkansas.net/encyclopedia/entry-detail.aspx?entryID=510. Michael Zimmer noted: "We saw a lot of General Siegel's monuments, that is ruins of houses which Siegel had had burned down." Macha and Wolf, *Michael Zimmer's Diary*, 153.

85. Mills were important to both armies as a means of producing flour and meal, but as the war progressed they were increasingly destroyed as Confederates sought to deny their use by Union forces or Federals burned them to keep them from being used by guerrillas. See Michael A. Hughes, "Wartime Gristmill Destruction in Northwest Arkansas and Military-Farm Colonies," *Arkansas Historical Quarterly* 46 (Summer 1987): 167–189.

86. The village of Maysville in Benton County was located on the border of Indian Territory, west of Bentonville, and just a short distance from Fort Wayne. *Arkansas* (Map), (New York: J. H. Colton and Co., 1855).

Nov. 3rd we proceeded to about 4 miles from Bentonville and camped on a farm. "Camp Bonne" it was called. A young artillery Lieutenant of the Second Indiana was careless enough to get into a love affair with a young lady and was encouraged. He went to see her, all alone but carried his arms. One day the young lady took his sword and revolver. Upon signal of her mother about half a doz. Guerillas stormed into the home, caught the unarmed lieutenant and took him out, tortured him in the most barbaric manner and buried him under dry leaves, where his comrades found him. When he did not return, his comrades, suspecting evil, investigated and found the corpse. The home of the girl with all the belongings was burned in retaliation. What became of the two women I had never learned.[87]

On the day we arrived at Camp Bonne, we and company P. and two Howitzers of the 2nd Kansas cavalry under Capt. Hess's command,[88] were ordered to Elm Springs[89] and arrived there at night. We were quartered in the many abandoned little houses. The town is named after the great springs issuing under an elm tree. A good water mill is at the place and we kept it going. The wheat is gathered from the farms of the community. We built ovens and soon bread was coming forth. Our real mission is advance guard, for there are rebels about and here they had a large drill ground. We have much picket duty.

Nov. 15th we marched again. We passed a mill which had been held by another regiment, in the morning the other regiment moved

87. First Lieutenant Matthew H. Masterson of the Second Indiana Battery, a native of Salem, Indiana, who had just received his commission on October 10, 1862, was killed by guerrillas at Spavinaw Creek, Arkansas, on November 1, 1862. *Report of the Adjutant General of the State of Indiana*, Vol. III—1862–1865 (Indianapolis: Samuel M. Douglas, State Printer, 1866), 387.

88. Gumal Hesse of Milwaukee enlisted in the Ninth Wisconsin on October 26, 1861, serving as captain of Company H. He transferred to serve as captain of Company B on December 5, 1862, where he served until being promoted to lieutenant colonel of the Forty-fifth Wisconsin Infantry on September 24, 1864. It is likely that it was Company B that took part in the expedition to Elm Springs, since there was no Company P. *Roster of Wisconsin Volunteers*, 608, 625.

89. Elm Springs is located just south of the Washington County line southwest of Bentonville. *Arkansas* (Map), 1855.

on for about a mile, as advance guard, and we remained. The Captain of our company was a very unfriendly man (a little devil and was hated by all). To fulfill his will we were to build an absolutely not needed fortification. When it was almost finished we found a Sign-board with a bulls head and two large horns and the inscription: "Fort Horn" the mockery in it was that the captain's name was "Horn."[90] In his anger he tried very diligently to find the originator of the sign but he knew that no one would betray him. Another incident I shall not mention. After a few days we left and went to our comrades at camp Babcock.[91]

Nov. 27th we all departed and came to Cincinnati—an insignificant town but it had a Tannery.[92] Going on we had to climb a very high mountain-like hill and the road full of pebbles. Then down again and to another small town with a great steam mill. The town was called Reas Mill, after the owner of the mill.[93] We marched through this town and then again climbed a high hill. Then we heard the sound of heavy guns and hurried forward.

90. Charles E. G. Horn enlisted in Company D of the Ninth Wisconsin Infantry on September 10, 1861, and was named first lieutenant on September 22. He was promoted to captain of Company A on April 18, 1862, and served in that position until being promoted to lieutenant colonel of the Second Missouri Volunteer Infantry of African Descent on February 20, 1864. *Roster of Wisconsin Volunteers*, 606, 614.

91. The Ninth Wisconsin moved to Camp Babcock on November 15. Major Schlueter noted in his diary that "Mr. Babcock was Beef contractor for Genl. Blunts command & otherwise connected with him – at that time he had enough money made & gave up the business." Herrmann Schlueter Diary.

92. Cincinnati was located northwest of Cane Hill near the border of the Indian Territory. The tannery would not survive the Union expedition into the area. John H. Kitts of the Eleventh Kansas Cavalry wrote, "I went out with a party about eight miles and burned and destroyed a large tannery....We took the hides from the vats and threw them into the house and sheds, and set fire to the buildings." Kitts valued the destruction of the Cincinnati tannery and another one nearby at $20,000. Shea, *Fields of Blood*, 76–77.

93. William H. Rhea owned the mill at Rhea's Mill, and Union troops occupied the site during the months of November and December 1862. After the war, Rhea unsuccessfully billed the U.S. government for expenses and damages from that occupation, claiming $680 for November and at least $1,030 for December. The mill burned after the battle of Prairie Grove and was later rebuilt. The mill's fifty-two-foot sandstone tower was moved to the Prairie Grove battlefield in 1958 and still stands on the grounds of Prairie Grove Battlefield Historic State Park. "Rhea's Mill," *Flashback* 7, no. 4 (December 1962), 16.

Soon we arrived at Cane Hill where the second brigade had encountered rebels and driven them back. Several of our men were wounded.[94] We camped in town. There were churches and stores and a lovely town it must have been but the people had fled. The next morning we returned to Reas Mill, where we camped for some days.[95] The mill was operated for our use. Wheat was gathered, ground, baked and eaten. The Cherokee Indians were with us—these days—under their Captain, Colonel Phillips.[96]

A New Order and Attack.

On Dec. 5th general Blunt[97] gave order to march but little was done and we were in suspense. At last, on the 7th, at sunrise we moved forward toward Cane Hill. Everything of our wagon was left behind. At

94. Brigadier General James G. Blunt led part of his Kansas Division in a nine-hour, twelve-mile running battle from Cane Hill through the Boston Mountains on November 28, 1862, driving Brigadier General John S. Marmaduke's Confederates back to Dripping Springs near Van Buren, Arkansas. Blunt lost nine killed and 32 wounded, Marmaduke about the same. Blunt returned to camp at Cane Hill, setting the stage for the battle of Prairie Grove. William Shea, "1862: A Continual Thunder," in *Rugged and Sublime: The Civil War in Arkansas*, ed. Mark K. Christ (Fayetteville: University of Arkansas Press, 1994), 48. For a detailed account of the action at Cane Hill, see Shea, *Fields of Blood*, 92–108.

95. According to Herrmann Schlueter, the Ninth Wisconsin set up camp at Rhea's Mills and commenced guarding the army's wagon train on November 29, but were prepared to be called to action: "Dec. 3—struck tents at 7 a.m. Brigade was ready to march. pitch tents again at 5 p.m. 4th Same as Yesterday teams laden at 6 a.m. 5th Same and stood under arms all day." Herrmann Schlueter Diary.

96. Colonel William A. Phillips, a former New York Tribune reporter and Kansas free soil backer, commanded the Third Indian Home Guard, which included many recruits from the Cherokee territory. He would later lead the entire Union Indian Brigade. The Third Indian was organized in June and July 1862. Clarissa W. Confer, *The Cherokee Nation in the Civil War* (Norman: University of Oklahoma Press), 78, 83; Frank Wilson Blackmar, *Kansas; a cyclopedia of state history, embracing events, institutions, industries, counties, cities, towns, prominent persons, etc. ... with a supplementary volume devoted to selected personal history and reminiscence*, vol. 1 (Chicago: Standard Publishing Co., 1912), 917.

97. Maine native James Gilpatrick Blunt, a physician and former ship's captain, moved to Kansas in 1856 to fight with the free soil forces there. The combative Blunt rose to the rank of major general in the Civil War and led his troops to victory in Arkansas, Missouri, and the Indian Territory. Steven L. Warren, "James Gilpatrick Blunt," *Encyclopedia of Arkansas History & Culture*, http://www.encyclopediaofarkansas.net/encyclopedia/entry-detail.aspx?search=1&entryID=5767.

Cane Hill—on a high hill—we formed battle line. Soon we heard the sound of artillery. But according to sound, the enemy moved toward Reas Mill. Quickly General Blunt gave orders to return and he himself raced back and the cavalry after him. Artillery stormed after them and all the infantry followed coming to the prairie, near Reas Mill our cavalry saw the great provision train, in best order arranged along the edge of the timber and protected by strange cavalry. They were our troops, just arrived from Springfield Mo. It was general Heron's Division, who had just arrived and met the rebels who were marching to attack our train. He attacked at once, as we heard at Cane Hill. Neither we nor the rebels knew then Gen. Heron was so close. The rebels would have surely captured our provision train, if Gen. Heron would not have saved the day.[98]

Battle at Prairie Grove.[99]

We were ordered to remain to guard the train at Reas Mill, with a Battery and a regiment of cavalry.[100] The rest of all the forces went

98. Brigadier General Francis J. Herron's Missouri Division marched 110 miles in three days to reach the Prairie Grove battlefield from Springfield, Missouri—a feat historian William Shea describes as "one of the extraordinary events of the war and an epic of human endurance." Shea, "1862: A Continual Thunder," 52. Francis J. Herron was born in Pittsburgh, Pennsylvania, on February 17, 1837. A banker before the war, Herron fought at Wilson's Creek and received a Medal of Honor for his actions at Pea Ridge. He was commissioned a brigadier general on July 16, 1862, and was promoted to major general—the youngest to reach that rank on either side at the time of his commission—on March 10, 1863, in recognition of his performance at Prairie Grove. He later served in Mississippi, Texas, and Louisiana. The former general died in a tenement in New York City on January 8, 1902, and is buried in Calvary Cemetery on Long Island in New York. Warner, *Generals in Blue*, 228–29.

99. Major General Thomas Hindman led the Confederate First Corps of the Army of the Trans-Mississippi into the battle of Prairie Grove, arranging his troops on high ground above the Illinois River. Fierce fighting started on the Confederate right, where Herron's Missouri Division of the Army of the Frontier attacked after its grueling march from Springfield. Blunt's Kansas Division entered the fight later in the day, hitting the Confederate left in desperate battle until night fell. Though he still held the high ground as night fell, Hindman's battered army, low on ammunition, fell back toward the Arkansas River Valley that night. For a succinct account of the battle, see Shea, "1862: A Continual Thunder," 50–57; for a riveting account of the entire campaign, see Shea, *Fields of Blood*.

100. The troops guarding Blunt's trains at Rhea's Mills included the Ninth Wisconsin Infantry, the Third Indian Home Guard, and the Twenty-fifth Ohio Battery. Britton, *The Union Indian Brigade*, 149; Banasik, *Reluctant Cannoneer*, 86.

after the enemy, who, though fighting, was in retreat towards a better position. There they took stand. Evening and night came and
still cannon roared and 4 miles away we could see lightning from
the guns. The fighting was on higher ground and therefore readily
seen by us. General Heron's troops were over tired and could not
resist much longer.[101] Now our artillery under Gen. Blunt came in
and with them came new courage. The Indian battery played havoc
among the rebels.[102] The rebels made three attacks against our artillery but at least they had to abandon their plan under terrific
losses. Now the rebels asked armistice to bury their dead. It was
granted to rest arms until two o' clock next day and then again to
open battle.[103]

We did not guard our train very long. The same night our entire
train was ordered to Tythville.[104] We arrived there at midnight and
remained till daybreak and then we proceeded toward the battlefield,

---

101. The savage fighting around the Borden House on the Union left had ravaged
Herron's division, already weakened by men who fell by the wayside on the march
from Springfield. Hindman had just ordered troops from his left to wheel to the right
and crush Herron when Blunt arrived on the field. Shea, "1862: A Continual
Thunder," 54–55.

102. Blunt fielded twenty artillery pieces of various sizes when he opened fire on
the Confederates at Prairie Grove. Haas is referring to Rabb's Second Indiana Battery
and its four six-pounder James rifles and two six-pounder guns. Rabb answered the final
Confederate attack of the day with canister, writing that "for fifteen minutes my men
stood firm, firing their pieces with terrible precision"; an admiring Iowa soldier wrote
that the Hoosier battery "appeared to be in one constant sheet of flame, so rapid were
the discharges." Shea, Fields of Blood, 218, 237.

103. Though Hindman's army had already started its retreat, at around 3 a.m.
on December 8, Brigadier General John S. Marmaduke requested a "personal in-
terview" between the commanders of the two armies to arrange a truce.
Marmaduke and Hindman met with Blunt and Herron between 9 and 10 a.m. that
morning, arranging a six-hour ceasefire. The opposing commanders also mutually
agreed that the battle would be called "Prairie Grove," the only time in the Civil
War that an action was named by mutual consent of both sides. Shea, Fields of
Blood, 245–46.

104. Major Schlueter wrote that "at 11 P.M. were ordered to escort train to
Fayettville. The whole train put in Motion for Fayettville, Washington C. Ark."
Herrmann Schlueter Diary.

which was about 18 miles away.[105] When we arrived at 2:00 p.m., the time set to re-open battle, we saw batteries, cavalry and long lines of infantry—all was ready. In the valley were several farms and wooded hills and our forces on the hills to the right. We waited but the enemy had withdrawn. They had muffled their artillery and the feet of the horses with blankets to avoid noise. Their train they had burned and had abandoned their wounded and dead. The enemy lost about 3,000 in dead, wounded, and missed. Many of their men deserted and came over to us, our own losses came to about 1,000 all told.[106] We buried the dead from both sides and the wounded were taken under care of physicians.

On the battle field stood a house in which women and children were in the cellar during the battle. The battle over, the woman came out and found the husband, brother and brother-in-law among the dead. Her grief was terrible. She blamed only us for the war. Soon after, her house burned with all that was in it. She had nothing left.[107] We remained on the battle-field until the 10th and then returned to Reas Mill.

105. Schlueter wrote that "at 2 o c A.M. orders came to report with the whole Regt. To Genl. Blunt, at the Battlfield before daybreak[.] Reported accordingly and were placed with 2 sections of Atillery behind Gen. Blunts Hd. Quarterz." Herrmann Schlueter Diary. Michael Zimmer held that the Ninth Wisconsin had marched nine miles toward Fayetteville when the order to return came and "we turned on our heel and arrived at dawn, but were very tired and sleepy." Macha and Wolf, *Michael Zimmer's Diary*, 158.

106. Official reports state that Hindman lost 204 killed, 872 wounded, and 407 missing, though the actual number could actually be higher. Federal losses are listed as 175 killed, 813 wounded, and 263 missing. Many of the Confederate "missing" were unwilling conscripts who deserted, some of whom later joined Union outfits. Shea, *Fields of Blood*, 261–62.

107. At least seventeen civilians sheltered in the cellar of the Morton House during the battle, emerging unharmed after the fight to find the yard filled with dead and wounded soldiers. A woman who found her husband and two brothers among the Confederate dead screamed, "Oh it was them God-damned federals that killed you, I wish they were in hell!"; one soldier reported that her shrieks could be heard across the valley. While the Morton House survived, Union soldiers burned the Borden, Thompson, and William Rogers houses on the day after the battle. Shea, *Fields of Blood*, 263–64.

I have omitted and now desire to give the strength of the opposing forces. We had about 23,000 men. The rebs claimed 30,000 but it seems they did not have more than about our number.[108]

Expedition after Van Buren[109]

We now camped and rested at Reas Mill until the 26th. Then orders were received to have rations for 6 days, to carry the rations for 3 days and have the other 3 days rations conveyed after us. Early on the 27th we left, leaving all unnecessary baggage behind. We went in hurried marches. Soon Cane Hill was behind us. We climbed high mountains up and down and saw but few homes. Soon we came to Boston Mountains and here proceeded along a road through the heart of the mountain, following a meandering creek. Roads became impassable and we had to take the creekbed going in cold and deep water. Twenty-three times we had gone through the water and there seemed to be no end.[110] Night came on and we made camp on a small farm. The fence rails served for thousands of camp fires. What a vision that was! Next day the wading through the creek began again. Knee deep and later deeper. Thirteen times we have been in—so far—today. Now two rivers meet and we have to go in again. It was deep and the current was so strong that we could hardly keep on our feet. It was the last crossing but it was the 37th time in 36 hours.[111]

108. Hindman's First Corps of the Army of the Trans-Mississippi contained about 11,500 troops, while the divisions of the Army of the Frontier at Prairie Grove numbered between 7,500 and 8,000 men. Shea, *Fields of Blood*, 261.

109. After learning that John Schofield was returning to take command of the Army of the Frontier, Blunt, and Herron decided to make a forced march through the rugged Boston Mountains to strike the defeated Confederate army at Van Buren, located north of the Arkansas River across from Fort Smith. See Shea, *Fields of Blood*, 268–82.

110. Michael Zimmer wrote on December 27 that "the road was very bad, we had to wade the same river 17 times. It was very cold and covered with ice, but not strong enough to carry a man, but it was not very deep, about 2 feet," while Herrmann Schlueter wrote that the troops had to march "through that G. D. D. creek (cove creek) 30 times during the day and the boys were perfectly worn out that night." Macha and Wolf, *Michael Zimmer's Diary*, 161; Herrmann Schlueter Diary.

111. Zimmer and Schlueter reported crossing Cove Creek twelve and seven or eight times, respectively, on December 28. Macha and Wolf, *Michael Zimmer's Diary*, 161; Herrmann Schlueter Diary.

Here is the Telegraph Line from Springfield to Van Buren. The forces under General Heron are here. We proceeded along the Telegraph Road. Up and down we went until we were on top of the mountain. Here it was more level and the country more inhabited. Gen. Blunt with the cavalry ahead of us. He surprised a rebel camp and captured two cannon and their provision train.[112] The rebels fled but soon we heard the voice of a cannon. We learned that the rebels, in greatest fear, had crossed the Arkansas River and left the City in our hands. We captured five steamboats.[113] Most of the citizens had left town.[114] We were still several miles from town and so tired that we could hardly walk nor stand and many fell down by the wayside but by and by they trundled after us.

Slowly we moved on and by night came to town. Each took care of his self best he could. Next morning a camp was chosen and the town inspected. I had just gone into a large store, many others were in and plenty of sugar there. We took some and we saw General Blunt enter. Gun in hand. The men fled. The general closed and locked the door.[115]

112. Blunt led the Second, Sixth, and Ninth Kansas Cavalry Regiments and three battalions of the Third Wisconsin Cavalry ahead of the rest of Army of the Frontier, slamming into and scattering Crump's Texas Cavalry in their camp at Dripping Springs. Shea, *Fields of Blood*, 271.

113. The Federals captured the steamboats *Frederick Nortrebe*, *Rose Douglas*, *Violet*, and *Key West*, as well as the ferryboat across the Arkansas River. Shea, *Fields of Blood*, 273–74.

114. Van Buren was not completely empty, Michael Zimmer observed, writing, "I strolled through the town which I liked a lot, but it was like a ghost town, because everyone had fled, but no, I met a citizen when I went into a nice house, but he was not alive, instead lying dead in a coffin, whereupon I left the place." Macha and Wolf, *Michael Zimmer's Diary*, 161.

115. Ohio artilleryman Robert McMahan was also in the warehouse. He wrote that "the building was filled with artillery men, infantry & cavalry men from day light up to 9 when Blunt made his appearance revolver in hand and drove us all out!!! Just dropping of goods and skedaddling!! But he had given time enough." Banasik, *Reluctant Cannoneer*, 98. Zimmer noted that the Yankees took what they wanted while in Van Buren: "We went into several houses and found lots of food: sugar, molasses, flour, whiskey, and many other things. We live here in the lap of luxury." Macha and Wolf, *Michael Zimmer's Diary*, 161.

The town is fine, all brick buildings, but is not a large town. It is situated on the Arkansas River and very large hills are on the opposite side.
A troop of negroes was found locked up in a barn, and anxiously peering
at us through the cracks. They told us their masters had locked them up
and told them to be very quiet. They were told the yankees would kill
them if they would find them. We set them at liberty and for joy they
jumped like crickets. Afterward they went with us.[116] We captured a rebel
provision train with the entire conveying force. They had no idea that
we were there and when they found out it was too late for escape.

On Dec. 30th we departed. The cavalry burned and destroyed all
ships and stores.[117] We marched back in hurry and came to the place
where we so bitterly crossed the waters. Here we killed cattle and
roasted meat, for we had nothing to eat. Now we were refreshed and
strengthened. We proceeded but not along the terrible waterway. One
river we had to cross but quickly a bridge was built. Then, at once, we
began to climb upward, as if we intended to climb up to heaven. At
least 1,500 feet we ascended. We were now on top of the Boston
Mountains. From now on we remained on the high plateau. There are
few homes because it is all rocks and hills and canyons. On Dec. 31st
we came to Prairie Grove and were cordially received by the 20th
Wisconsin regiment.[118] We were tired and hungry. We were quartered

116. Around 500 slaves seeking freedom followed the Army of the Frontier from
Van Buren. Shea, *Fields of Blood*, 280.

117. In addition to the four steamboats and ferry boat, Blunt estimated that the
Federals burned 20,000 tons of corn and tons of other supplies as they left Van Buren.
Shea, *Fields of Blood*, 280.

118. Herrmann Schlueter wrote on December 31: "Resumed March at day break
& marched to the late Battlefield of Prairie Grove found the 20th Wis. Col. Bertram
and Said Regt. invited our boys to stay with them which was cheerfully accepted."
Herrmann Schlueter Diary. The Twentieth Wisconsin Infantry was organized at
Madison, Wisconsin, and mustered in on August 23, 1862. The regiment suffered 49
percent casualties, much of it in savage fighting around the Borden House, during the
battle of Prairie Grove, losing 50 killed, 154 wounded, and 13 missing. The Twentieth
would later serve in Mississippi, Louisiana, Texas (including an incursion into Mexico),
and on the Alabama Gulf Coast. The regiment lost 105 men killed or mortally wounded
and 146 to disease before mustering out on July 14, 1865. Dyer, *Compendium*, 2:1682;
Shea, *Fields of Blood*, 180.

in the tents of that regiment and rested well. In this expedition we had marched 120 miles.

Beginning of 1863.

On the first morning of the New Year we had our breakfast with the 20th regiment. Then, soon the trumpet called us to rally. Soon we were in line. Then several "Hurrah" were given the 20th regiment for their hospitality and after this we hurried away toward Reas Mill. There we rested until next day. Then the entire command marched and on the third day we came to Elm Springs. Here camp was made and soon a general review of all the troops under General Schoefield was held.[119] On January eleventh we all left and in the same night came to the prairie at Bentonville and here in the comfort of fence-rail fire, rested a while. On the 12th we proceeded to the Telegraph Road and from there to Cross Hollow—a deep ravine crossing the road. Here, to please travelers, feed troughs have been placed along the water front. We turned to the left— following the ravine—and soon came out of the timber, to a clearing, where we found a very fine large spring. From this the water was led to a water mill. Here we rested. A multitude of small chimneys told us that here the rebels must have had their winter quarters.[120] A very high hill is at our right and another at the left. After a short rest we again marched and soon came to another mill. From here we soon came to the White River, which is wide but not very deep at this place. We waded through and on the other side made camp till morning. At day-break we marched into the mountains. Soon we crossed the War Eagle Brook. We climbed up a high hill and then had deep ravines on both sides. Soon the country became more inhabited and we saw much fine oak timber. Eight miles from Huntsville we made camp, on a large farm, in a deep valley.

119. The parade was held on January 6, when Michael Zimmer wrote: "Today regimental parade. Weather a bit better." Macha and Wolf, *Michael Zimmer's Diary*, 162.

120. The Confederate Army of the West had established winter quarters at Cross Hollow, located on the Telegraph Road sixteen miles north of Fayetteville, but abandoned and burned the camp on February 19, 1862, for fear of being flanked by the Union Army of the Southwest. Shea and Hess, *Pea Ridge*, 38, 48.

The country along White River is very romantic. There are deep ravines and very high rocky banks of the river. In the bottom lands are very productive but mostly small farms, between high mountain walls. Here are excellent hiding places for criminals, rebels and bushwhackers. Valleys are connected by brook or river every time. Often such valleys—rough and rocky—are not inhabited.

We made this expedition to cut off the retreat of the rebel General Marmaduke and his band, who was driven out of Missouri. Marmaduke became aware of the trap, took another route and escaped.[121] Here we remained for some time. One morning we had about 4 or 5 inches of snow but this soon disappeared.

On Jan. 18th we broke camp. Roads however were so bad that men were delegated to assist the provision train, two men to each wagon. Progress was very slow. If one wagon pulled out of the mud, another got into it and sank to the ooze deeper than the first. Often it took 6 to 12 mules to pull a wagon out. The entire day we only made 5 miles. At such work we grew exceedingly hungry and opened barrels and boxes and helped ourselves. We made camp and fence-rails supplied bed and fuel. Fence-rails as bed kept us from sinking into the mud and the fire at our feet kept us comfortable. So we rested splendidly. Next day it was the same terrible task—mud and water—but by evening we reached better road, near War Eagle Camp, where we had been once before.[122]

Jan. 20th. We went to the creek but could not cross because of flood water. So we had to make camp to wait or try and find another road. We tried to make a bridge, by cutting and dumping in trees, but

121. Brigadier General John S. Marmaduke led a force of between 4,000 and 6,000 men against Springfield, Missouri, where about 1,000 convalescent soldiers, militia, and Unionist civilians held them off on January 8, 1863, suffering 14 killed, 145 wounded, and five missing. Marmaduke's force fell back to Arkansas that night. OR, 22, 1:10.

122. Herrmann Schlueter wrote on January 18: "Companies ordered to help teams through the mud.... [M]arched all day, or rather waded in the mud," and on January 19, "roads horrible—marched a few miles, halted went back to help wagons out of the mud." Herrmann Schlueter Diary.

the current was too strong. All attempts failed. We had to wait. On Jan. 22nd we crossed the now much lower creek. The water went into the wagon boxes, but all went well. A large Mill had burned but the well-built water Dam was in good condition and the water rushed over.[123] Some of our forces had crossed the river before the flood, in another place. On the same day we went on and crossed the mountain. We entered a deep valley and came to a recently built mill. Here we made camp. The mill was equipped with fine machinery for sawing, grinding wheat and all kinds of work a mill might be expected to do. A large spring at the foot of the mountain gave the water power.[124] Next day we marched on over the top of the mountain, saw poor country and had bad roads. At last we came to the White River and now we had to make a neck-breaking descent, into the river bottom. Here we met the rest of our forces. These were engaged in building a Flatboat to cross the river. Some of the wagons and artillery had been brought across both sides at night, to give light and aid in the task. A large rope was now stretched across the river and the flatboat was pulled back and forth.[125]

On Jan. 25th we at last went over, took up the heavy rope and began to climb on over bad roads and wild country. At night we came

123. This was the War Eagle Mill on War Eagle Creek. Charles Lothrop, *A History of the First Iowa Cavalry Veteran Volunteers, From Its Organization in 1861 to Its Muster Out of the United States Service in 1866* (Lyons, IA: Beers & Eaton, 1890), 83.

124. This was Peter Van Winkle's mill, which the Van Winkles had abandoned when they fled to Texas with their slaves in 1862, after which it burned. The remains of the mill site are interpreted at Hobbs State Park–Conservation Area near Rogers, Arkansas. Katherine Cleek, "Van Winkle Mill Site," National Register of Historic Places nomination, Arkansas Historic Preservation Program, Little Rock, 2007. Surgeon Lothrop of the First Indiana Cavalry referred to it as "Rip Van Winkle's Saw Mills." Lothrop, *History of the First Iowa Cavalry*, 83–84.

125. Michael Zimmer wrote that construction of a ferryboat began on January 21, but the initial attempt was abandoned after it sank the next day with the regimental adjutant and several officers aboard, who "were drifting downstream in next to no time, accompanied by loud laughter." Herrmann Schlueter also noted on January 22, "Raft was ready but proved to be a failure down the river it went." The troops marched to another spot on the White River where a raft was built successfully and the command crossed the river on January 24 and 25. Macha and Wolf, *Michael Zimmer's Diary*, 163–64; Herrmann Schlueter Diary.

to Elk-Horn Tavern. Low, in a sunken road, we made camp. The tavern we found in ashes.[126]

Jan. 26th. In rain and snow we came to Kittsville. We found quarters in the many empty houses. The next day we marched through the little town of Heasville,[127] went through and camped on the edge of a timber. Here bread was baked for we had flour. Leaving Cassville,[128] we again entered the state of Missouri and left Arkansas.

Jan. 28th. We marched all day, mostly through timber and here and there past a home. In the evening we made camp on the bank of Green Creek, in dense brush. There were plenty of fence-rails. That gave us wood for our campfires. It was very cold in our tents. We tarried in Camp Green Creek until Febr. 21st. On that day we moved on 20 miles and then camped on a large cultivated prairie. There was a large white house and people in it. The second day brought us to Mount Vernon. A nice town with many brick houses and a Court House.[129] This was occupied by State Militia.[130] There were many stores but most of them closed or abandoned. We went on for some miles, and at last, in rain and snow, made camp in a bush. It was called Camp Soloman. Here our comrades, who had been captured in the battle at Newton, came

126. The Federal troops who had established a post at Elkhorn Tavern were ordered to Prairie Grove on December 14, 1862. Bushwhackers burned the building soon afterward. A new Elkhorn Tavern would be built in 1885. A. W. Bishop, *Loyalty on the Frontier or Sketches of Union Men of the South-West with Incidents and Adventures in Rebellion on the Border*, ed. Kim Allen Scott (Fayetteville: University of Arkansas Press, 2003), 57; Shea and Hess, *Pea Ridge*, 327.

127. Michael Zimmer's entry for January 26 says "camped at Kezville where we quartered in houses," and on January 27, he wrote "passed the village of Haysville." Macha and Wolf, *Michael Zimmer's Diary*, 166.

128. Platted in 1845, Cassville was the county seat of Barry County, Missouri. The town served as the Confederate capital of Missouri for one week in 1861, and was occupied by both sides during the war, most frequently by Union troops. Earngey, *Missouri Roadsides*, 41.

129. Mount Vernon was platted in 1845 and served as the county seat for the newly formed Lawrence County, Missouri. Earngey, *Missouri Roadsides*, 185. Haas apparently liked the area and would settle there after the war.

130. This was most likely the Fourth Missouri State Militia, which had a detachment ordered to Mount Vernon on August 20, 1862, and was reporting from the town as its headquarters on September 27, 1862. *OR*, 12:587, 676.

back to us. They had been set free in exchange for Southern prisoners.[131] We now built ovens and baked bread.

On March 2nd. We—company A. and company I.—with two Howitzers and cavalry were ordered to Bower's Mill, a little town.[132] We had to proceed over prairie and then, for a while, through timber until we came to a valley and river, where the mill stood. The town is close by. We took position on a high hill, overlooking the town and community. We went out to get wheat, ground it. We made ovens and baked bread. It was forbidden to butcher swine, but we did. Many people brought butter, eggs, pies and other things and we bought of them, but money was scarce for we had not received pay for a long time. Our old disgruntled Major[133] wanted to build fortifications but little was done because we soon moved on.

Stone (Gravel.)

On March 19th we again took the road. We came back to Mount Vernon but by a different route. Here we met our regiment and together marched till evening and then made camp at the bank of a river. Next day we came through a country covered with little stones. It was poor ground and all the timber was dwarf-like.

Before long we reached the Telegraph Highway, from Springfield. At a large spring we made camp. The third day we came to a country where everything was white—covered with white round stones, about the size of a hen-egg. You could not set a foot on ground except you stood on such stones, nor could grass grow through them.

131. The winter quarters for the Ninth Wisconsin were at Stahl's Creek, 36 miles west of Springfield, Missouri, and that is where the paroled Newtonia soldiers joined them. Quiner, *Military History of Wisconsin*, 543.

132. Bower's Mill was located west of Mount Vernon near the Lawrence/Jasper county line. *Johnson's Kansas and Missouri* (Map), (New York: Johnson and Ward, 1864).

133. Herrmann Schlueter of Milwaukee was major of the Ninth Wisconsin at this point, having been promoted to the position on August 14, 1862, from captain of Company E of the regiment. He would muster out of the regiment on December 3, 1864, when his term of enlistment expired. Schlueter mentioned in his diary that Companies A and I were sent on detached duty at Bower's Mill, but did not mention going with them. *Roster of Wisconsin Volunteers*, 604.

The James River and The Ozarks.

All day we marched until toward evening we came to a valley, all around hedged in with steep and almost sky-high rockwalls. Here, in the canyon-like valley, we made camp. Mountain high walls were all around us and the James River in front. White Sycamore trees are all along the river's bank. Here are splendid hiding places for criminals and bushwhackers.[134]

On March 20th we went on, crossed mountains and again came to the James River. Then in an open place we camped. We remained until March 22nd and then crossing mountains and valleys, we came to Helena,[135] a little town in exceedingly rugged country. The James River deep below, passes the town. This nest was occupied by militia.[136]

March 23rd. We proceeded and again crossed mountains and twice we crossed the James River. Here the river was not deep and all crossed on cavalry horses. Horses balked, objecting to carrying two. One horse, two men on it, got into deep water and turned over but all came out except one gun which remained in the river. This wilderness is little inhabited only a recluse here and there. It seemed to be almost apart from the world. After a march of about 14 miles we came to a deep, rocky ravine, with high walls around. Here was a house with many women in it. They were much frightened and at the same time surprised and in-

134. Robert McMahan of the Twenty-fifth Ohio Battery wrote, "The 1st high bluff on South side of river and above camp had harbored a nest of marauders high up in a cave where the Ks. 10th found a shotgun, blanket, hams and cornbread also boiled ham and cornbread. The gentlemen had left rather suddenly and whether in the rear of the cavern or somewhere else no one could tell though search was made until after dark, blankets were taken out and burned." Banasik, *Reluctant Cannoneer*, 130.

135. Haas is referring to Galena, the county seat of Stone County. The county was organized in 1851, and the seat was originally to be named Jamestown, but that was changed to Galena in 1853 in recognition of the lead ore in the sparsely populated county. Earngey, *Missouri Roadsides*, 98.

136. Three companies of the Fourteenth Missouri State Militia had garrisoned at Galena from June 29, 1862, until shortly before the Ninth Wisconsin passed through the town, when two companies left. Robert McMahan of the Twenty-fifth Ohio Battery wrote, "There is a company of milita stationed here, about 40 in number under command of Capt. White." *OR*, 13:457; Banasik, *Reluctant Cannoneer*, 132.

terested over such company. They thought here they could never be found and had never seen so many men together.

On March 24th we came to a country more mountainous than ever. On the crest of this mountain we marched for a long time. We had a clear vision of the country for 20 or 30 miles around. It was mountain peak after mountain peak. Five or six of them are deep crevices and rocks. Here and there a crippled bush or dwarf-tree. We saw no game, no animal. We meandered over the mountain in winding roads best we could until at last we came to a down-ward sloping country. Then we saw the White River before us. Here we made camp and again saw dwellings of men.[137]

The White River

On the second day of our White River Camp some were sent out after feed and provision, about 4 or 5 men to each wagon.[138] Two wagons were ordered to go to a side road. I was on one of these wagons. The others went straight down to cross the river. We tried to cross the river near our camp. The river here was wide but not deep. The mules showed little liking for the water. One of our men waded ahead of them and then the mules followed. When the water became deep the man came into the wagon, but the mules bravely brought us over. Soon we came to a house and barn, found corn, loaded our wagon and proceeded toward our camp. We men sat in the wagon on top of the corn. When we came to about mid-river, our two small lead-animals came into soft ground. Soon they could not stand in the deeper water and began to drift and kick, and pulling the other four mules along down stream. They became mixed up in the harness and the danger of drowning was

137. Herrmann Schlueter noted that this camp was at the "White River opposite mouth of King's River." Herrmann Schlueter Diary. Robert McMahan observed, "Family living here on the bottom in an old loghouse....Boys pitched in and the chicken and geese and some little bacon were soon sacrificed to appease the wrath of our hungry stomachs." Banasik, *Reluctant Cannoneer*, 133.

138. Two companies of the Ninth Wisconsin accompanied the Third Wisconsin Cavalry on this 104-man foraging expedition. Banasik, *Reluctant Cannoneer*, 133.

on. We tried to climb out along the wagon tongue, among the struggling animals, to cut the harness. The tongue had been bent downstream and the lower wheels were sinking in loose ground. Our wagon was now in danger of turning over. Water was ready to flow over corn and wagon and we had to be ready to jump.

The four front mules had been washed away. One of them came out living, the other three drowned. The last two larger mules we got out. The river was about 160 feet wide and deep in some places only. Our precarious situation was seen from camp and some of our cavalry, with large horses, came to our rescue.

The wagon with corn was finally salvaged. A rope was attached to the tongue of the wagon and then mules pulled it out. The second wagon was brought over with great caution and successfully. The other wagons—the river rising—could not be brought over that day. That evening the regiment moved farther down river. Our company A, and some cavalry had to remain to await developments of the wagons on the other side of the river. Next morning they and we, on opposite sides of the river, too moved downstream. We went down about six miles and camped under large trees, aside of a great rock wall. The regiment, on a circuitous route, came to us later. Now a flat-boat was built and all went over. The river was much lower now and wagons and horses could cross. We were eight miles from the Arkansas line. Sycamore, oak and ash were prevailing in the woods.

March 23. We went forward over rolling country and came to Berryville,[139] a very small town. We camped on an open field and went

139. Colonel William Weer, commanding the First Division of the Army of the Frontier, led a force of the Ninth Wisconsin Infantry, Third Wisconsin Cavalry, and Twenty-fifth Ohio Artillery to Arkansas to attack Confederate troops gathering on Crooked Creek between Carrollton and Yellville. OR 22, 2:183–84. Berryville, located in eastern Carroll County, was founded in 1850 and had a post office established there on July 13, 1852. The town suffered heavily during the Civil War, with only three buildings surviving when hostilities ceased. Cindy Williams, "Berryville (Carroll County)," *Encyclopedia of Arkansas History & Culture*, http://www.encyclopediaofarkansas.net/encyclopedia/entry-detail.aspx?search=1&entryID=842. Both Schlueter and McMahan wrote that the expedition reached Berryville on March 29. Herrmann Schlueter Diary; Banasik, *Reluctant Cannoneer*, 134.

on next day and came to Carrolton,[140] a good sized town surrounded densely with young oak timber. It was so dense that sometimes you could hardly see 10 feet ahead. We camped near town, on open field. After we had camped here for several days, at different times guns were fired from dense woods at some of our soldiers and one was wounded.[141] This caused great irritation among the men. Several companies of cavalry were sent out with orders to burn every house in the community. Orders were carried out quite promptly and some of the suspected people were shot.

April 6th we left Carrolton and much of the city was burned in reprisal of the deeds of Bushwhackers. On April 9th we marched on the crest of a hill, covered with pine wood, and came to Forsyth at the White River.[142] The town is in the bottom on the East side of a high hill. With a flat-boat we crossed the river and passed several fortifications built by the 19th Iowa regiment who had camped here for some time.[143] We camped at a brook emptying into the White River. Behind us was the valley, before us Forsyth—a little town of about 12 houses, with Courthouse in center, on a very level plot of ground. At our left

140. Carrollton was first settled around 1833 and became the Carroll County seat, with a courthouse built around 1836. By 1860, the prosperous town had a population of around 2,000. Mike Polston, "Carrollton (Carroll County)," *Encyclopedia of Arkansas History & Culture,* http://www.encyclopediaofarkansas.net/encyclopedia/entry-detail.aspx?search=1&entryID=6192. Carrollton had already suffered considerably when the expedition arrived. Robert McMahan wrote: "This town has been quite a prosperous place but is now nearly deserted. The brick court-house is burned down and the walls are not more than 3 to 5 ft. high, rubbish and broken bricks lying all round." Banasik, *Reluctant Cannoneer,* 136.

141. Michael Zimmer wrote on April 1: "Today we got the news that our teamster Iahn Kraemer was shot into the lower abdomen by a bushwhacker, but it is not dangerous. He had gone out to get some fodder for his team." Macha and Wolf, *Michael Zimmer's Diary,* 169.

142. Forsyth was platted around 1836 and was named the seat of Taney County. A brick courthouse was constructed in 1855. Earngey, *Missouri Roadsides,* 92–93.

143. The Nineteenth Iowa Infantry was stationed at Forsyth from February 15 to April 22, 1863. The regiment was organized at Keokuk and mustered in on August 25, 1862. It suffered 55 percent casualties at Prairie Grove, losing 45 killed, 145 wounded, and three missing of the 350 men who entered the battle. The Nineteenth Iowa mustered out on July 10, 1865, having lost 92 men killed or mortally wounded and 100 to disease. Dyer, *Compendium,* 2:1172–73; Shea, *Fields of Blood,* 181.

was a steep high hill, near the Camp, at least a 200 feet straight rock wall and rising higher farther back. We found that the country here too was troubled and infested with guerrillas. Soon we found that three men of the Third Wisconsin Cavalry had been murdered.[144] Reprisal will surely follow.

April 20th. We received orders to pack everything we cannot carry into the wagons, which is to be sent to Springfield but to retain rations for 5 days. We still remain with some cavalry and our ever accompanying Battery, for which the rebels have shown great respect. After noon we moved on just one mile and then rested along a fence, on a fine, about 8 feet wide, space, under large trees and the artillery behind us in the field. From green boughs, we made tents. On April 22nd we left our bivouac, climbed up a large hill and from here saw, in the direction of Forsyth, a very dense black smoke. "Forsyth is in flames" everybody said and surely it is a reprisal for the deeds of the guerrillas. We marched on through very wild and rough country.

Spirited Pursuit.

We were marching quite unconcerned on the crest of the upland, sensing no danger. A few prisoners marched in the rear. Then suddenly a gun shot and more musket firing. Looking back we saw wild excitement. The entire left wing of the regiment ran and fired down the hillside and we at the right wing had no idea what was going on, but each clutching his gun. Cavalry clattered down the hill. Soon it became known that only one of the prisoners tried to escape. That man had his gall with him. Seven bullets in him he still fought a cavalrist who had him by the collar.

---

144. Charles W. Porter of the Third Wisconsin Infantry wrote in his diary on April 18: "On my arrival [in camp after detached duty] I learned that two of Capt. Offs Co. 'K' had been found killed and laying in the road about 14 miles from camp. More informal work of guerrillas but we get in some good work with them to make up for our loss." Charles W. Porter, *In the Devil's Dominions: A Union Soldier's Adventures in "Bushwhacker Country"* (Nevada, MO: Bushwhacker Museum, 1998), 60. The dead men were Joseph Bohnert and Conrad Stegmann, who were listed as "Killed April 14, '63, while carrying dispatches, Ark.," *Roster of Wisconsin Volunteers*, 120, 122.

A bullet into his head made him quiet. We marched on and soon came to a large spring, below green trees, and here we made camp.[145]

The Ozarks.

On April 23rd we came to the little, insignificant town "Ozark." The most important is a long, build-over bridge, across the river. At the bridge is a mill near which we halted to rest.[146] Soon we crossed the bridge, marched about five miles farther and camped in an open field. We had no tents.

The Thunderstorm.

After we had settled down, and no one to contest our being here, the heavens made array and marshaled against us. Clouds like a great mountain chain, black and threatening, mutteringly marched toward us. Fence-rails are the soldiers' feather-bed and fuel. We quickly gathered them, hardly had we provided for our needs when heaven's artillery let loose and the pillars of the earth were trembling. When the storm giant had passed us the great black mountainous clouds over us began to weep, almost drowning us and nearly washing us away, and roaring over us like angry gods. We stretched out upon improvised beds, pulled our wax-linen over and let the waters under the fence-rails sing our lullaby, grumbling and muttering. Finally the storm passed on but looked as threatening and black from the rear as from the front. Our little human fires (Camp-fires) had been quenched by heaven's tears, but we revived them again.[147]

---

145. Michael Zimmer wrote of the incident: "A prisoner escaped, but was hit by several bullets. He fell to the ground and died. He was an old man and would have been released tonight. So he was buried near the camp." Macha and Wolf, *Michael Zimmer's Diary*, 170.

146. Joseph Kimberling established a mill at Finley Creek in 1833, and a community grew around it. Ozark was platted in 1843 and when Christian County was organized in 1859, it became the county seat. Earngey, *Missouri Roadsides*, 200–201.

147. Michael Zimmer wrote that the storm hit at 2 a.m. and "entirely soaked us." Macha and Wolf, *Michael Zimmer's Diary*, 170.

Next day we again took the road but four men were ordered to go with each wagon because of the difficulties of the road. Whoever got stuck had to see how they would get out. Others would drive by, wagons with good mules had the better part.

On the afternoon we came to White Oak Springs. Here a large Spring issued forth from a large White Oak and taking the name therefrom. After resting a while, we proceeded over winding roads. Late in the afternoon we came to a deep valley, and there found other troops camping. Here we found our tents and wagons dispatched from Forsyth. We joined with our friends in camp.[148]

The next day we moved on. The roads still so very bad and each wagon had extra men delegated. It was impossible to proceed in line. We went through timber, making front of about half a mile. Sometimes what was to be the rear was in front. Some of us reached the little town of Hartsville but when evening came, the most of the regiment stuck in the mud behind.

At Hartsville we made camp in the Courthouse. This Courthouse was riddled by cannon balls and on the inside, books and furniture were scattered in wildest manner. This good sized town had a very poor location. From a very steep hill you get into town and steep hills are all around. A small brook and river run by. All looks dilapidated and most houses are empty.[149]

On April 27th our other forces arrived. We had, by this time, made a long bridge across the brook. Here we all crossed and after going a mile and a half came to the Gasconade River. This river is wide and deep, but we tried to make a bridge. We cut logs and let

148. Herrmann Schlueter wrote on April 26: "Train with Regt. train could not follow on account of the bad road & stuck in the mud." Herrmann Schlueter Diary.

149. The Hartsville area was settled in 1832 and platted in 1841 to serve as the seat of Wright County. Earngey, *Missouri Roadsides*, 113. Confederate and Union forces clashed there on January 11, 1863, in the last battle of General John S. Marmaduke's first Missouri raid, a daylong fight that caused 78 Union and 11 Confederate casualties. Banasik, *Reluctant Cannoneer*, 145n. Robert McMahan wrote: "Hartvile [sic] like all the other little villes of Mo. is nearly used up, only a few families live here. The community was nearly all secesh." Banasik, *Reluctant Cannoneer*, 146.

them fall into the river. We had almost reached the middle of the river.
I stood, farthest out. Now a very large tree was cut and I saw that it
would fall in the very place I stood on a log, in the river. Quickly I
had to jump and dive under the log I stood on. The big tree crashed
in where I had been and its branches into the water around me. I
crawled out, unharmed but as wet as a water mouse. I went to the
shore, undressed, wrenched my clothes, put them on again and stood
by the fire until dry. The men went to another place where there was
an island in mid-river and here at last we succeeded in making a
bridge. Then all returned to town and next morning company A.
crossed over and went four miles ahead. There, on a farm, we waited
for our regiment. Soon they came and we were on the march again.
Next day April 27th we kept on the march and toward evening came
to Houston and there, on a creek bank, made camp.

Houston.

Houston is a fine, inviting small town with many stores and brick
houses, but these are mostly empty, and many in ruins.[150] Many small
huts, chimneys and fire places indicated that troops were here in winter
quarters.[151]

Salem.

On April 20th [30th] we left Houston. Our company A. was in
the rear end and made ourselves comfortable by hanging everything
on the wagons and marched behind. We were in pinewoods on high

150. Houston was platted in 1846 as the seat of Texas County and named in honor
of Sam Houston. It was destroyed twice during the Civil War. Earngey, *Missouri
Roadsides*, 120. Robert McMahan observed: "This was quite a place, had over 40
houses, but now not over half a dozen are occupied by citizens." Banasik, *Reluctant
Cannoneer*, 147.

151. Houston had been occupied by the Fifth Missouri State Militia Cavalry and
Third Iowa Cavalry prior to April 1863. McMahan wrote: "No troops here at present,
but a large number have been, judging from the camping grounds." Banasik, *Reluctant
Cannoneer*, 147.

ridges and in the evening made camp in the woods. On the third day—May 1st—we came to Salem. It is a medium sized, very busy town.[152] We camped on the edge of a small creek, fed by a large spring. On the one side was beautiful oak timber and from the branches we built protection against the hot sun. On the fine level ground, several times, we had drill.

Rolla.[153]

On May 5th company A was ordered to the 25 miles distant, larger town Rolla. We had to take the empty train for all kind of repair. We made 15 miles that day and then made camp in dense woods, at a small lake. The next day we passed the camp of the division on the way to Rolla. In this division we found the 20th regiment, who at once recognized us and asked many questions. Without stopping we went on through the camps to the different regiments. At last we came to a prairie. Here we saw large herds of mules guarded by a number of men.

Soon after, we came upon a bleak hill. From the top, close to the road, we saw a cemetery with many, many small crosses and many of them had picket fences around. At the left, not far away was the Fort with several large cannon upon the rampart.[154] Troops were in the Fort, and not very far away was the town with a fine Courthouse. To our right was the main town and R.R. station. From here several trains, daily, made connection with St. Louis. It is

152. Salem was settled in the 1830s and platted in 1851 as the Dent County seat. Earngey, *Missouri Roadsides*, 242. Michael Zimmer described it as "a very nice town." Macha and Wolf, *Michael Zimmer's Diary*, 171.

153. Rolla was established in 1855 when the Pacific Railroad built offices and warehouses midway between St. Louis and Springfield, Missouri. Two years later, the town was platted to be the seat of Phelps County. Rolla became a major Union stronghold during the Civil War. Earngey, *Missouri Roadsides*, 220–21.

154. Colonel J. B. Wyman and the Thirteenth Illinois Infantry occupied Rolla on July 6, 1861, establishing a permanent U.S. presence in the town. The Thirteenth Illinois began construction of a large fortification, which was completed by other units and named Fort Wyman. *OR*, 3:391; information found at Rolla Area Chamber of Commerce, http://www.rollachamber.org/moving-to-rolla/history-of-rolla.

mainly transportation for the army. It is a growing and seemingly prospering town. We made camp between Fort and Courthouse. We were at leisure and often went to town, to the courthouse and to the Government Wagon Factory.

We remained until May 24th and lived well. Had plenty of beer etc. On that day we left Rolla, without train, and went back to the camp of the 20th regiment. Next morning, early, we were on the march again and about evening came to Salem, and on the same day we received our pay. During our stay in Rolla, the Governor of Wisconsin[155]—brother of our Captain Solomon—came on a visit. From here he went to the regiment to Salem to enquire into the status of the troops. The Governor inspected the regiment, we had drill and he, in a speech, gave high approval of what he saw.[156] At the same time the Generals Schoefield and Heron were present. Such drills and inspections are pleasure for the visitors but very hard work for the soldiers. We rebuilt tents, ovens etc. and made our camp more comfortable, but when we had everything in good shape order came and we had to leave.

On June 5th tents were taken down and put on wagons. Knapsack on back and gun on shoulder we were off on the road toward Rolla. Rain had fallen and progress was slow. It was late when we reached the old campground of the 20th regiment. The 20th was gone. We set up our tents and slept well. On the morning of June 6th we proceeded about 3 miles from Rolla and there awaited further orders. The 10th,

155. Edward Salomon was born in Strobeck, Prussia, on August 11, 1828, but fled to the United States in 1849 after supporting the 1848 German uprisings. Salomon settled in Manitowoc, Wisconsin, in 1852. Elected lieutenant governor in 1861, he assumed the governorship after Governor Louis P. Harvey drowned on April 19, 1862. Salomon returned to Germany in 1894 and died in Frankfurt-am-Main in 1909. "Salomon, Gov. Edward," *Dictionary of Wisconsin History*, http://www.wisconsinhistory.org/dictionary/index.asp?action=view&keyword=Edward+Salomon&term_id=2686.

156. "G.," a correspondent for the *Wisconsin State Journal*, wrote that during Governor Salomon's visit "the 9th regiment gave an exhibition of their proficiency in skirmishing and other drill, and received a merited compliment from their commanding General." Quiner Scrapbooks, 3:5. Robert McMahan noted that Salomon "made the 9th Wis. a German speech." Banasik, *Reluctant Cannoneer*, 157.

11th and 12th Kansas regiments are here in camp not far away.[157] Heavy
rains made mud deep and we had to change camp.

Rolla.

On June 14th we received order to move into town. The 10th
Kansas camped close to us. We made tabernacle of branches, had much
drill but a good time.

July 4th 1863.

The day began with a greeting from 34 large cannon. In the afternoon Grand Review under General Davis.[158] This closed with another
bark from the 34 cannon, and then, tired and overheated, our company
rested, and refreshed itself with two barrels of beer.[159]

157. The Eleventh Kansas Infantry was organized near Fort Leavenworth between
August 29 and September 14, 1862. The regiment served in the Indian Territory,
Missouri, and Arkansas before being mounted and designated the 11th Kansas Cavalry
in April 1863. The erstwhile infantry regiment would muster out on September 26,
1865, after losing 61 men killed or mortally wounded and 112 to disease. Dyer,
Compendium, 2:1184, 1188. The Twelfth Kansas Infantry was organized at Paola in
September 1862 and served in Kansas, Arkansas, and Missouri. When it mustered out
on June 3, 1865, the regiment had lost 12 men killed and mortally wounded and 123
to disease. Dyer, *Compendium*, 2:1188–89.

158. Brigadier General Thomas Alfred Davies assumed command of the District
of Rolla on March 13, 1863. OR, 22, part 2:154. Born December 3, 1809, in St.
Lawrence County, New York, Davies graduated from West Point in 1829. Leaving the
army in 1831, he rejoined the army when the war began. After serving in Virginia,
Mississippi, and Kentucky, he commanded the District of Rolla in 1862 and 1863, end-
ing the war in command of the District of North Kansas. He received a brevet promotion to major general in 1865 and spent his later years writing books. He died in St.
Lawrence County on August 19, 1899. Warner, *Generals in Blue*, 113–14.

159. Michael Zimmer describes the July 4 review thus: "Today the 9th Wisconsin
and the 10th Kansas had to fall in. Then General Daewis [sic] had the cavalry attack
us with drawn swords and thought they could break through our lines, but it turned
out differently. When our Colonel saw them attacking, he ordered: Form square! Which
happened immediately, and the second command was: Charge bayonets! Whereupon
the cavalry turned on their heel, and the horses galloped away so that their riders lost
their caps. Weather hot." Macha and Wolf, *Michael Zimmer's Diary*, 174.

General Inspection.

On July 6th, with knapsack on our backs we were inspected by General Jotten.[160] This officer was very meticulous and painstaking and long before he was through, marching orders came. Then he had to hurry to finish his inspection, to our great joy. Then all became quiet and we did not march out.

On July 7th again inspection, and at this occasion General Grant's victories were read to us.[161] Loud Hurrahs shook the air. The cannons— 34 of them—roared, and then we went to our camps.

July 8th orders came to take the train for St. Louis, and at once. We proceeded to the station and after waiting a while boarded the train. We stopped a little while at Franklin and then went without interruption until we reached St. Louis. We marched through the city to Camp Edwards (sometimes called Jackson)[162] where under beautiful trees on a green lawn we made camp. Soon women and children came to sell

160. James Totten was born in Pittsburgh, Pennsylvania, on September 11, 1818, and graduated from West Point in 1841. A Mexican War veteran, Totten surrendered the U.S. Arsenal in Little Rock to the State of Arkansas in February 1861, commanded an artillery battery during the Camp Jackson affair in St. Louis in May, and received promotion to lieutenant colonel after his performance in the August 10, 1861, battle of Wilson's Creek. Totten, a hard drinker, served in the Army of the Frontier until March 21, 1863, at which point he became inspector general of the Department of Missouri, serving in that capacity until August 6, 1864. Totten was made a brigadier general in the Missouri Militia in 1861 but was never promoted in the U.S. Army, though he did receive a brigadier's brevet on March 13, 1865. Totten died on October 2, 1871, at Sedalia, Missouri. Banasik, *Reluctant Cannoneer*, 289–92.

161. Michael Zimmer wrote on July 7: "Today the news arrived that Vicksburg has been take[n] and that General Lee has been defeated....We had a great review and several speeches were made." Macha and Wolf, *Michael Zimmer's Diary*, 175.

162. Camp Jackson was located on the western edge of St. Louis. It was the base for the city's secessionists in the tense days that followed the attack on Fort Sumter and was named for Missouri's secessionist governor, Claiborne Jackson. On May 10, 1861, 6,000 Unionist volunteers led by U.S. Army captain Nathaniel Lyon surrounded the camp and ordered its surrender. Following the surrender, a pro-secessionist crowd gathered and after one of the Unionists was mortally wounded, the others opened fire, killing twenty-eight people and wounding many more. The Camp Jackson affair led many Missourians to throw their support to the Confederacy but kept the St. Louis Arsenal in U.S. custody. Information found at missouricivilwar150.com.

all kinds of things to eat. Here we enjoyed rest. Fuel, water, and bread were brought to us.

On July 13th our company A. was given the watch of the town. And we were quartered in a 5-story building, in the center of the city, near Linden Hotel, which was not fully completed. We soon found that our rooms were alive with all kinds of vermin. Without hesitation we went for water and brooms and then beginning in the upper story made a thorough cleaning. For days we worked and washed and scrubbed until uncounted regiments of bedbugs were eliminated.

Often we had to break up night-parties. Sometimes we arrested and penned them up and next day took them home. Theaters and Goblinghouses[163] likewise had to be looked after. Street riots were not allowed.

To enable us to speedily go to distant parts of the city, 20 horses were at our disposal. Whenever disreputable persons were apprehended we turned them over to the Provost Marshal.

Our entire regiment had been quartered in the surrounding Fort and Barracks. Several companies were put as guards into the Mc Dowall College, to guard the rebel prisoners kept there.[164] Soon however we were delegated to guard another—a state prison—where soldiers and criminals were kept.

We now were in the Schoefield barracks No. 4 and close to us was company F. These barracks were well arranged. All are three-story single beds. Kitchen and dining are in good condition and good water close at hand, supplied from the city water works every other day we had to be on duty. Soon we had to do duty at the College, which is a strong, 4-story stone building. The windows are barred with iron and it looks much like a fortress. It was filled with rebels.

163. This is probably referring to gambling houses.

164. Haas is referring to the Gratiot Street Prison, located at 8th and Gratiot streets and located in the former McDowell Medical College building. Information found at www.civilwarstlouis.com.

The Rats.

The nights brought much diversion because of the great multitude of unusually large rats. They were almost countless in number, and so annoying that they ran over our feet. They were in every house and even upon the roofs. At night, on the sidewalks, they would run under your feet and squeak all around you. When on guard-duty we would throw wood and stones at them, even use the bayonet. If you scared off one, two or half a dozen would be behind you or between your feet. It was aggravating and highly irritating.

Enmity—Marching Orders.

At this time the First Nebraska regiment arrived at St. Louis, but in such dilapidated condition that we laughed at them.[165] This, naturally, was resented and bitter feeling arose and became more aggravated from day to day. Soon they were given Provost Guard, and now had the right to arrest any without a pass, and did so to the utmost in respect to our men. The most of the citizens, because of our order and good behavior, preferred our men and were, therefore, often abused and mistreated by the Nebraskans, and even shot at.

At one time, when many of us were in a Concert Hall, a strong patrol, armed, came in to arrest our men. They took some of our men. The others slipped out of the back-door. They followed to apprehend them, outside, and when they escaped shot after them. This made matters worse and after this fights occurred at different times, in diverse places. Men equipped themselves with revolvers and knives and carried

165. The First Nebraska Infantry was organized in July 1861 and served in Missouri, Tennessee, and Mississippi before being stationed in St. Louis in August 1863. The regiment was ordered mounted on October 11, 1863, and became the First Nebraska Cavalry, which would see extensive action in Arkansas. It mustered out on July 1, 1866; Dyer does not list casualties. Dyer, *Compendium*, 2:1344-45. The First Nebraska Infantry included one company, Company B, that was enlisted primarily of German immigrants. One can wonder whether these were the men for whom the Ninth Wisconsin felt such enmity. James E. Potter and Edith Robbins, eds. *Marching with the First Nebraska: A Civil War Diary* (Norman: University of Oklahoma Press, 2007), xix.

bayonets. This was against the law and things became worse every day. Then all at once, orders came that our regiment had to leave. This was fortunate because serious clashes were almost sure to come.

Sept. 12th. With knapsack ready we stood out on the street at headquarters. Our guns were stacked orderly, on the streets, and we were allowed to rest. At the end of our right wing was a saloon, just on a street where some of these Nebr. scamps had their quarters. Some of our men went into the saloon to get a drink. Some of the Nebraskans were in and at once began to mock our men. Some of our officers and men attacked and flailed them and cast them out of the saloon. They escaped but defiantly hurled back some rocks. Some of their ilk hurried up to help them but abstained when they saw the great number of our men, ready to go for them.

Leaving St. Louis—The Mississippi.

It took the greatest effort of our officers to keep our men from attacking the Nebraskans. The entire regiment was angry, and great harm could have easily been done. Soon the bugle called and we left in best order. We marched through the city, passed the Courthouse and into 4th street. The streets were filled with men and women. Our regiment, because of good order and behavior, had the good will of the entire population of the city. We were about 700 men. Soon we reached the river and embarked on the streamer "Mars."[166] New Orleans was our destination.

---

166. The Mars was a 329-ton sidewheel paddleboat built in Cincinnati, Ohio, in 1856. Confederate forces had seized it at Memphis in June 1861 and pressed it into service. U.S. troops captured it at Island No. 10 on the Mississippi River on March 7, 1862, finding it heavily vandalized. After major repairs, the Mars went to private owners who ran it between Memphis and the Ohio River, then on the Missouri River. The Mars sank at Cogswell Landing, Missouri, on July 8, 1865, after hitting a snag. Frederick Way Jr., Way's Packet Directory, 1848–1984: Passenger Steamboats of the Mississippi River System Since the Advent of Photography in Mid-Continent America (Athens: Ohio University Press, 1994), 309.

The Mississippi

Sept. 12th, in the afternoon, we left St. Louis, but only went to Corondelet. We disembarked and remained on shore for the night.[167] On the 3rd day—Sept. 12th—we reached the Great Bend, at Cape Girardou, but passed on without delay. At 4:00 p.m. we reached Cairo, Illinois, where we stopped and remained until the next day.[168] Here the Ohio River entered into the Mississippi. The Ohio's water is green, that of the Mississippi is yellow. The river is full of sand mostly coming from the Missouri River. Here at Cairo three states meet: Illinois, Missouri, and Kentucky. From there the Central R.R. runs to Chicago and another road to St. Louis. Many steam boats and Cannon Boats are at anchor.

Sept. 15th 1863 Early in the morning we went down to the river, and at 11:00 a.m. came to Columbus. We reported our arrival and then went on. Columbus is a military station and has a strong and well-manned fort on a high hill. This controls the river.[169] Soon we passed Island No. 10., well known because of the heavy fighting for its possession.[170] It is a triangular

167. Carondelet, Missouri, along with Cairo and Mound City, Illinois, and Cincinnati, Ohio, was a center of Union gunboat construction during the Civil War. Gary D. Joiner, Mr. Lincoln's Brown Water Navy: The Mississippi Squadron (Lanham, MD: Rowman and Littlefield, 2007), 18.

168. Located at the confluence of the Ohio and Mississippi Rivers, at the start of the Civil War, "Cairo was the most strategically important real estate on the North American continent, excluding the District of Columbia." Cairo became a major Union naval base and the place where many of the ironclad gunboats that fought on western waters were built. Joiner, Mr. Lincoln's Brown Water Navy, 14–26.

169. Columbus, Kentucky, on the Mississippi River was the western anchor of Confederate defenses that stretched from there to the Cumberland Gap in 1861. Confederates abandoned the heavily fortified stronghold after U. S. Grant's victories at Forts Henry and Donelson in February 1862, and Federal troops seized Columbus on March 2, 1862, without a fight. It remained in Union hands for the duration of the war. David S. Heidler and Jeanne T. Heidler, eds., Encyclopedia of the American Civil War (New York: W. W. Norton and Co., 2000), 471–72.

170. The Confederates armed Island No. 10, located on the Mississippi River just south of New Madrid, Missouri, with 6,000 troops, 123 heavy guns, and 35 other pieces of artillery early in the war in an attempt to control traffic on the Mississippi River. Outmaneuvered by Union troops and ships, the garrison surrendered on April 8, 1862, opening the Mississippi south to Fort Pillow. See Jack D. Coombe, Thunder Along the Mississippi: The River Battles that Split the Confederacy (New York: Sarpedon, 1996), 85–94.

Island. Only a few soldiers and negroes living on it. In many places nearby we could see the remains of ships sunk in battle. The same is true all along the river.

Sept. 16th we passed Fort Tillon, likewise situated on a high hill.[171] Here the country is steep, rough and wild. Wild geese and ducks are in abundance. At 10:00 o'clock at night we came to Memphis, Tennessee. Here we remained till morning and went to see the town. We saw the fine public square, several hospitals and large business houses. President Andrew Jackson's statue, a fine marble monument, was much admired.[172] It is surrounded by a fine iron enclosure, and tables, benches and speakers platform are provided.

Sept. 17th we traveled on, and on the 18th at 11:00 a.m. we saw Helena in Arkansas. We came close to Helena and then, all at once, were tight on a sandbar, so tight that another boat had to come pull us off. Then we went to the shore and stopped.[173]

171. Early in the war, the Confederates had constructed fortifications at key points along the Mississippi River north of Memphis in an effort to control traffic on the river. Fort Pillow, 80 miles above Memphis, held at least twelve 32-pounders. The Confederates abandoned Fort Pillow on June 4, 1862, and Fort Randolph farther south the next day, opening the river to Memphis. *Official Records of the Union and Confederate Navies in the War of the Rebellion*, 30 vols. (Washington DC: Government Printing Office, 1894–1922), series 1, 4:408. OR, 10, part 1:901.

172. The bust of Andrew Jackson was located in Memphis City Park on the Mississippi River and was donated to the city by Joel T. Parish of Memphis. It was dedicated on January 8, 1859. Andrew Ewing, *An Oration Delivered on the Occasion of the Inauguration of the Bust erected to the Memory of Gen. Andrew Jackson in the City of Memphis, January 8, 1859* (Nashville, TN: E. G. Eastman and Co., 1859).

173. Michael Zimmer wrote: "Today at 10 o'clock we came close to Helena, but our steamboat ran aground on a sandbank, were we were stuck until 5 o'clock in the evening." Macha and Wolf, *Michael Zimmer's Diary*, 178.

Helena. [174]

When we came close to the shore many soldiers came and enquired whence we came and what regiment we were. We looked well and many took us to be conscripts but soon found out differently. Next day, when we left the steamer and marched through town, they saw us drill and kept quiet. We made our camp on the North side of the city, near the river and pitched our tents under trees, cleared the place and had a fine camp. The town is close to the river bank and does not amount to much. Most of the people live in small houses and are small merchants. Behind the town are high hills and upon these are Forts, occupied by soldiers. [175] Above Helena is much timber. The town is in a valley. Little breeze touches it and there is much fever, because of the river and swamps nearby. [176]

Two large Cannon Boats lay there, idle, because the river was low and shallow, they could not proceed until a rise in the river would come. These cannon boats, in the battle in July, inflicted great damage to the rebels. [177] Steam-boats, cannon boats and iron clads come and go daily. The shores are sandy, and often great banks, with timber on, fall into

174. The Helena area was settled around 1815 and the town incorporated in 1831 as the seat of Phillips County. General Samuel Curtis's Army of the Southwest occupied Helena on July 12, 1862, and the town would become a major Union base on the Mississippi River for the remainder of the war. Steven Teske, "Helena-West Helena (Phillips County)," *Encyclopedia of Arkansas History & Culture*, http://www.encyclope-diaofarkansas.net/encyclopedia/entry-detail.aspx?search=1&entryID=950.

175. The approaches to Helena were protected by four batteries, designated A, B, C, and D, on the high ground above the city. Edwin C. Bearss, "The Battle of Helena, July 4, 1863," *Arkansas Historical Quarterly* 20 (Autumn 1961): 267.

176. Helena was notoriously unhealthy for the troops stationed there, and poor water and inadequate sanitation led to epidemics of malaria, typhoid, and dysentery. One soldier claimed that "it is almost sure death to at least 1 out of 3 of all unacclimated persons who come here, except late in fall or in winter." Christ, *Civil War Arkansas, 1863*, 106.

177. A Confederate army attacked Helena on July 4, 1863, and was repulsed, with heavy casualties. The Union defenses were bolstered by the timberclad gunboat USS *Tyler*, whose commander reported firing 433 shells during the battle. The Confederate army of 7,646 men suffered 1,636 casualties; the Union garrison of 4,129 only 220. Christ, *Civil War Arkansas, 1863*, 116–44.

the river, and sand and timber drift downward and often block the river. Ships there often need repair and these cannon boats have to stand guard that rebels may not destroy the ships during repair. One ship was in flames, when we passed by. The river, all along, shows the signs of ruin and devastation of the war.

Oct. 5th 1863. Our company made a pleasure trip down river. We are to guard the boats against guerrillas. We went about 30 miles and then landed to make contract for delivery of wood for the government boats. This accomplished, we returned. The fine weather made it a pleasure trip.

After the great and unfortunate battle at Chatanooga, boat after boat passed here, often 6 to 14 larger and smaller, with troops of different kind on them. It was to re-enforce our forces, and to finally overcome the rebels.[178] We saw more than 12,000 men pass by. Many of the regiments in camp here were ordered to follow. Among them was the 12th Wis. Battery, which just lately had arrived from Vicksburg.[179] We spend much of our time bathing and swimming in the Mississippi. At this time much sickness appeared in our regiment. Over 100 men, including myself, were sick with chills and fever. On October 10th, our regiment proceeded by land, leaving the sick and unnecessary baggage behind, to be brought after them by steamboat. I still was with the sick.

The Trip by Steamboat.

On Oct. 11th the expected boat came to our camp. Soon, all that remained of our regiment was brought on board. Our beds went below into the engine room, among much baggage. All was open and often we were unpleasantly cool, but we tried to bear and be patient. The two

178. The Union Army of the Cumberland fell back to Chattanooga, Tennessee, following its defeat in the September 19–20, 1863, battle of Chickamauga, Georgia. The Confederate Army of Tennessee besieged the Union troops until being driven back into Georgia in late November.

179. The Twelfth Wisconsin Battery was organized at St. Louis in February and March 1862 and would serve in Mississippi, Tennessee, Alabama, Georgia, and North Carolina. The battery was in Helena on September 12–27, 1863. The Twelfth Wisconsin Battery lost 11 men killed or mortally wounded and 23 to disease during the war. Dyer, *Compendium*, 2:1673.

upper decks were occupied by the sick of another regiment and were in no better condition. We left the same day and by noon of the 13th we were at the mouth of the White River, where we had to remain until a cannon boat came down the White River. The scenery along the shore was much the same, only in the state of Mississippi were more of the large slave plantations, with their many negro huts. Here, at the mouth of the White River we see nothing but a few negro huts. These negroes here cut wood for the river boats. Generally several gunboats are here and keep watch. As soon as a boat appears and does not report, there is a boom and a cannon ball roars over it. No report now and another ball follows. No boat except a friendly, then comes closer. Most of them quickly turn. If the boat is fast, it is sunk by cannon ball and the Captain is punished with a large payment for disobedience. We here took in wood and coal and remained until Oct. 15th. Then another boat came, took us on board and we proceeded up the White River. Soon we came to a very dangerous place in the river, where many logs blocked the way. It was only with greatest care we passed. Here we found the wreck of the steamboat "Lady Jackson" which often had given us pleasure with its whistle.[180] All that was valuable had been removed.

After passing this dangerous place we came to a tributary of the Arkansas River and now found fine passage and could proceed much faster and on the 19th we came to Clarenton, where we found our regiment in camp, waiting for us and to be set across the river. The long trip on the White River showed the shores covered with dense woods, the trees covered with vines and the shores generally low. The river is winding and has large bends. It is mostly deep water.[181] In day-time we

180. The *Lady Jackson*, a 207-ton sternwheel paddleboat built at Cincinnati, Ohio, in 1860, had mainly steamed on rivers east of the Mississippi. It hit a snag and was lost on the White River on October 14, 1863. Way, *Way's Packet Directory*, 275.

181. The White River, fed by the fast-moving, low-silt Black and Little Red Rivers, maintained a deep and clear channel that allowed it to accommodate larger and deeper-draft vessels than other rivers in the state, making the White the most important river in Civil War Arkansas. Bobby Roberts, "Rivers of No Return," in *The Earth Reeled and Trees Trembled: Civil War Arkansas 1863–1864*, ed. Mark K. Christ (Little Rock: Old State House Museum, 2007), 74–75.

traveled, at nights we had to lay by. A cannon shot from the boat was the sign, in the morning, for departure.

As soon as we landed, wagons and mules were taken on and conveyed to the other side of the river. Then the boat returned to get more. The next morning the rest of the regiment was brought over and off we went. Clarenton is a village in ruins. The people have left and only a few houses are intact.[182]

For a while now our boat proceeded between high, rough banks. Then we came into a corner-like bend and we were at Duvall's Bluff, our destination.[183] Farther boats do not go. It is the end of the boat-line. Here is the junction of the Boat-line and the Railroad to Little Rock.[184]

Duvall's Bluff & Little Rock.

Clarenton is small and unimportant but Duwalls Bluff is more so. We found hardly a single house. We saw nothing but tents along

182. Clarendon was designated the county seat when Monroe County was created on November 2, 1829, though the town would not be formally incorporated until February 8, 1859. Clarendon's location on the White River near the mouth of the Cache River made it an important White River port. W. R. Mayo, "Clarendon (Monroe County)," *Encyclopedia of Arkansas History & Culture*, http://www.encyclopediaofarkansas.net/encyclopedia/entry-detail.aspx?search=1&entryID=942. A Union soldier who had passed through Clarendon in August 1863 wrote that it "had only about fifty buildings, scarcely one of which appeared occupied. Windows had been broken and the ashes here and there told the tale of previous destruction." Christ, *Civil War Arkansas, 1863*, 158–59.

183. DeValls Bluff, located on the White River and on the eastern terminus of the Memphis and Little Rock Railroad, had been settled in the late 1840s. Major General Frederick Steele established a permanent base there in August 1863 during the campaign to capture Little Rock, and the river and railroad provided a dependable means of supplying the capital. Bill Sayger, "DeValls Bluff (Prairie County)," *Encyclopedia of Arkansas History & Culture*, http://www.encyclopediaofarkansas.net/encyclopedia/entry-detail.aspx?search=1&entryID=965.

184. The Memphis and Little Rock Railroad was the only railroad in Arkansas at the beginning of the Civil War, and, by 1863, only the section between DeValls Bluff and Huntersville (modern-day North Little Rock) was in operation. The strategically important rail line would be the frequent target of Confederate raids. Van Zbinden, "Memphis and Little Rock Railroad (M&LR)," *Encyclopedia of Arkansas History & Culture*, http://www.encyclopediaofarkansas.net/encyclopedia/entry-detail.aspx?search=1&entryID=2304.

the shore, occupied by soldiers. The R.R. station had been burned by rebels.[185] The day our boat arrived, our regiment likewise marched in and camped here over night, but went on the next morning. We—the invalids—had to leave the boat and to put our tents near the Rail Road Station, but when all was unloaded we entered into the R.R. cars.

On Oct. 20th at 2:00 P.M. we left and passed through a long prairie and then through bush and brush. For a short time we stopped at Brownsville, a little town in midst of the woods.[186] Toward evening we came near Little Rock, which was on the opposite side of the wide Arkansas River.[187] There was hardly a house on our side and we had to set up our tents to find shelter from the pouring rain. The next day our regiment arrived and at once marched into town and made camp on the South-side of the City.

On the 23rd we too went across the river and made camp near them. Close to our camp are the 29th Iowa and the 28th Wisconsin

185. Haas is mistaken. The railroad depot, along with rolling stock, at DeValls Bluff was destroyed by Union forces on an expedition up the White River on January 18, 1863. Mark K. Christ, "'Them dam'd gunboats': A Union Sailor's Letters from the Arkansas Post Expedition," *Arkansas Historical Quarterly* 66 (Winter 2007): 463.

186. Brownsville was founded to serve as the county seat shortly after Prairie County was created on November 24, 1846, though it was not formally incorporated until December 5, 1856, and the town boasted a population of around 2,000 when the Civil War began. The site of a skirmish on August 25, 1863, Brownsville faded away after the tracks for the Memphis and Little Rock Railroad were laid several miles to the south and the county seat was moved to DeValls Bluff after the war. Mike Polston, "Brownsville (Prairie County)," *Encyclopedia of Arkansas History & Culture*, http://www.encyclopediaofarkansas.net/encyclopedia/entry-detail.aspx?search=1&entryID=6088.

187. The first group of settlers in what became Little Rock moved there in the spring of 1820, and the Arkansas territorial capital was moved there from Arkansas Post in the fall of 1821. Little Rock was incorporated as a town in 1831, as a city in 1835, and became the state capital when Arkansas was admitted into the Union on June 15, 1836. Little Rock housed a provisional Unionist governor after Federal troops occupied the city on September 10, 1863, and the state's Confederate government moved to Washington in southwest Arkansas. James W. Bell, "Little Rock (Pulaski County)," *Encyclopedia of Arkansas History & Culture*, http://www.encyclopediaofarkansas.net/encyclopedia/entry-detail.aspx?entryID=970.

Infantry regiments.[188] The 27th Wis. is in camp West of the city.[189] Little Rock is a large city. There are churches and many small stores but most of them are empty and closed because the people fled when the city was taken. Many by and by came back. Goods have to be brought up from the Mississippi. Rebel boats had not been able to come up the river and prices were very high.

Many things could not be bought at all until ships took up the transport of goods. Jews and other profiteers soon took things in hand and charged enormous prices.

Provisions often could only be bought from military commissions, and citizens had to pay high prices. A barrel of flour would bring $24.00 to $28.00 and some times could not be had at any price. From 25 to 35 cents was the price of a small loaf of bread. It would not be enough for one man for one meal. The people had little besides the very coarse corn meal. Butter and eggs vary from 60 to 80 cents per lb. or per doz. and even up to a Dollar. The country people had been robbed of about everything and had little to sell.

Additional Account of the March to Little Rock.

As said before, our regiment left Helena on Oct 10th marched by land, mostly through cultivated country and much of it in timber. At nights camp was made. The second day the horse of our First

188. The Twenty-ninth Iowa Infantry was mustered in on December 1, 1862, in Council Bluffs and served the bulk of its service in Arkansas, participating in most of the major battles and campaigns of 1863 and 1864. The regiment lost 43 men killed or mortally wounded and 267 to disease. The Twenty-eighth Wisconsin Infantry mustered in at Milwaukee on October 14, 1862, and, like the Twenty-ninth Iowa, saw most of its service in Arkansas followed by posts in Alabama, Texas, and Louisiana. The regiment lost 13 men killed and mortally wounded and 227 to disease. Dyer, *Compendium*, 2:1175, 1685.

189. The Twenty-seventh Wisconsin Infantry mustered in at Milwaukee on March 7, 1863, and served at the siege of Vicksburg before crossing the river to campaign in Arkansas in 1863 and 1864. The Twenty-seventh lost 22 men killed and mortally wounded and 237 to disease. Dyer, *Compendium*, 1684–85.

Lieutenant[190]—which had been stolen the day before—was found in a stable, in the densest of timber. The day went by without trouble until toward evening. Then we saw smoke in the far distance and found that the bridge crossing a large creek had been set on fire, by bushwhackers, so as to keep our regiment from fast advance. In two hours a new bridge was constructed and the regiment marched on. After marching about two miles, these bushwhackers shot from hiding places, and then galloped away, and tried again at other places. But little damage was done.

On the third morning ten of our men were ordered to set fire to all empty houses around. Promptly they did so and that day we were not molested.[191] On the 4th morning all went well up to about 10:00 A.M. when these vile fellows fired again and a bullet went through the body of the horse of our adjutant and had to be killed.[192] At the same time they fired at our train. This irritated the entire regiment, and mainly the first lieutenant, who had the command of the regiment.

The first farmer, he happened to be a very old man, was brought before the Lieutenant, and was told in sharp words that dire reprisal would come upon him as soon as one other shot would be fired by

190. It is difficult to determine who Haas is referring to here, since there apparently was no one with the rank of first lieutenant of Company A, Ninth Wisconsin, in October 1863. Charles Frantz, who had been named first lieutenant of Company A on March 19, 1862, had been promoted to captain of Company G on November 27, 1862, and Adam Maass, Frantz's successor, would not be promoted to first lieutenant until May 11, 1864. *Roster of Wisconsin Volunteers*, 606, 611.

191. Michael Zimmer wrote that the houses were burned on the morning of October 13, and there was one shooting incident: "During this time someone shot at a comrade from our company who wanted to relieve himself about 50 paces from our camp. Fortunately the bullet only went through his trousers." Macha and Wolf, *Michael Zimmer's Diary*, 178.

192. Bernhard Hartfiel was appointed as sergeant major of the Ninth Wisconsin Infantry on October 4, 1861. He was promoted to second lieutenant in Company K on February 13, 1862, and transferred to Company B on September 30, 1862. He was promoted to regimental adjutant on July 16, 1863, and mustered out on December 3, 1864. *Roster of Wisconsin Volunteers*, 604, 608, 631. Michael Zimmer wrote of this incident: "We set off at 7 o'clock and did 3 miles, fetched fodder whereupon our adjutant was attacked by a bushwhacker. His horse was shot, but did not collapse which was his luck. It only collapsed when he had reached us and had to be killed." Macha and Wolf, *Michael Zimmer's Diary*, 178.

these scoundrels, and every house from Helena to Little Rock would be burned. The old man trembled all over, like an Aspen leaf, and left. After this, all during the march, not another shot was fired. In the evening the regiment reached Clarenton, where they then waited until we arrived with the boat and put them across the river. This was on the 17th. On the 18th they again marched and came to Duvall's Bluff. From there they left next morning, and on the 22nd, at 4:00 P.M. reached Little Rock. The march from Helena to Little Rock amounted to 161 miles.

New March.

Having made comfortable camp and some rest, unexpectedly new marching orders were received and early on the 26th of October we had to roll up our blankets and with rations for 5 days, be ready to leave.[193] All invalids—myself included—remained in camp, in tents. At 3:00 o'clock the entire Division of Infantry left. The cavalry had left earlier.[194] The artillery remained with the infantry. Good progress was made and by evening Benton was reached. There were many houses in good condition, but not all were occupied. The town is on a hill and surrounded by timber.[195] Here all rested for two days. Then the creek behind Benton was crossed and on the same day Rockfort was

193. On October 25, 1863, Confederate cavalry under Brigadier General John S. Marmaduke attacked the Federal garrison at Pine Bluff. After a day-long battle, the Confederates fell back after Colonel Powell Clayton's much-smaller Union force successfully barricaded the courthouse square with cotton bales and withstood the Rebel attack. For a succinct account, see Mark K. Christ, "The Federals Fought Like Devils," *North and South* 12 (March 2011): 40–48.

194. Lieutenant Colonel Henry C. Caldwell of the Third Iowa was ordered to bring a cavalry column to the relief of Pine Bluff on the morning of October 26. Brigadier General Samuel Rice was ordered to march an infantry brigade to Benton in support of the pursuit of Marmaduke's Confederates. OR, 22, part 1:728.

195. Benton was first settled in 1833 on the banks of the Saline River and became the Saline County seat after Arkansas became a state in 1836. A fortified Union outpost was established there in the fall of 1863. Patricia Paulus Laster, "Benton (Saline County)," *Encyclopedia of Arkansas History & Culture*, http://www.encyclopediaofarkansas.net/encyclopedia/entry-detail.aspx?search=1&entryID=979.

reached.[196] The river Washto runs by, close to town.[197] Camp was made under open sky. Heavy rains set in and by morning everybody was soaked to the skin. It turned cold. Fires were kindled but were of little use in the pouring rain. All waited impatiently for hot coffee to warm them. At last the voice of the cook sounded "Boys get the coffee or it will get wet." Jokes often help to break the terrible monotony and suspense in camp and on the march.[198]

At last, about 8:00 A.M., the signal was given to go forward, but we went back the way we had come. The Artillery, because of the muddy roads, often stuck in the mud and Infantry had to pull them through. Camp had to be made. The next morning, Oct. 31, the biweekly Inspection was made but not much attention was paid to strict order or cleanliness.[199] This over march was taken up and at 5:00 P.M. we were back at Benton. The next day our cavalry from Achedelphia, where they had scattered the rebels, and burned their Machine Factory and burned the Powder Mill arrived.[200] We had been ordered to assist them, in case of a battle, but our aid was not necessary now.

196. Rockport was established in the late 1830s and in 1846 became the county seat of Hot Spring County. The seat was moved to the railroad town of Malvern in 1879. Steven Teske, "Rockport (Hot Spring County)," *Encyclopedia of Arkansas History & Culture*, http://www.encyclopediaofarkansas.net/encyclopedia/entry-detail.aspx?search=1&entryID=6171.

197. This is the Ouachita River, subject to frequent misspellings in Civil War correspondence.

198. Michael Zimmer wrote: "We did 24 miles and came to Rockford, a village where we put up our camp in a field. It was easy to set it up well, as we did not have any tents with us. The earth was our bed and the blanket our only protection. The weather was very bad, cold and throughout the night it rained heavily, like a cloudburst." Macha and Wolf, *Michael Zimmer's Diary*, 180.

199. Zimmer would not agree with Haas's assessment, writing on October 31 "at 7 o'clock we had an inspection and indeed a great one, because I had to do the inspection." Macha and Wolf, *Michael Zimmer's Diary*, 180.

200. Caldwell reported that his cavalry arrived at Arkadelphia at 2 a.m. on October 29 and "at Arkadelphia I captured 2 lieutenants, some $1,370 in Confederate money, belonging to the Confederate Government, being proceeds of sale of Government salt; 3 six-mule teams, belonging to the Confederate Government; a large mail, and 8 or 10 Confederate soldiers." OR, 22, part 1:729.

The Provision Train.

Late in the evening we arrived at Little Rock. The distance from Benton is 25 miles and about the same distance to Rock Port. We traveled, going and coming about 100 miles. From now on, except for provision, no expeditions were made. Drill and campwork was our only exercise. On Nov. 17th, our company, with large empty train was ordered to Duvals Bluff, to seek provisions, because supply by R.R. was insufficient. At our destination we found mud and mud again. Heavy barrels had to be rolled in mud and other provisions carried until we had filled our wagons. Roads almost, it took us eight days to get back to Little Rock.

At different times other trains were sent out after corn, hay, oats etc. Generally about 100 wagons in a train. Often they were filled on one farm. Men simply entered the large fields and picked the corn. Most of the corn was in fields unpicked. The practice was to gather the corn the next year. The slaves had gone and crops were not harvested. Often we went 10 to 40 miles into the country and besides grain, ham, chickens and fresh meats were brought in. It was bought but generally not paid for. Hunger knows no law and especially not in time of war, in enemy country. The soldier generally feels quite at ease feasting in the enemy's cellar. Even the knapsack is filled and as much as possible put on the wagon. Other soldiers had to build a fort. About 200 men were at work daily, all through the winter, building, but Sunday was the day of rest. The Fort is on the Telegraph Road between here and Benton. It has the form of a square and is situated on a hill, far above the town.[201]

Re-enlistment.

During this month much was read to us about re-enlistment. It was made very important and we were urged to become veterans. Many enlisted again for three years. The promise was $400.00, which seemed much

201. This for was Fort Steele, located on the block bounded by Fifteenth, Sixteenth, Gaines, and Arch streets and covering the road to Benton. Construction of the fort began on November 9, 1863, and was completed by mid-December. Diane Sherwood, "Forts of the Civil War," *Arkansas Gazette*, magazine section, December 11, 1938, 1.

money at that time.[202] We were still obliged for another year and would be counted for one of the three to become a Veteran. A goodly number were willing to re-enlist. The New Year came on and only 118 had enlisted to become Veterans. From our company A. only eight had signed.[203]

The year 1864 began and the first act of great Importance was the execution of an enemy spy. He had been betrayed by a young woman.

The Spy.

On Jan. 8th 1864 a Southern Spy was hanged here in Little Rock. Many people witnessed the execution, but they were mostly blue uniform. The condemned was a young man in the twenties. Seated on a wagon on his coffin, he was brought to the place of execution. Arrived at the place, a clergy man led in prayer. The condemned wept but said that it was his own fault. He was a well dressed man and kept very quiet and cool. When he had nothing more to say the rope was laid around his neck and the wagon driven from under him. He dangled in the air and in ten minutes he was pronounced dead, put into the coffin and taken to burial. He had written to his mother and declared himself guilty.[204]

202. Veteran volunteers were experienced soldiers whose enlistments had expired who were enticed with furloughs and bonuses to re-enlist in the service. Webb Garrison with Cheryl Garrison, *The Encyclopedia of Civil War Usage: An Illustrated Compendium of the Everyday Language of Soldiers and Civilians* (Nashville, TN: Cumberland House, 2001), 256.

203. Correspondent "Appendix" wrote on January 11, 1864, that "over 200 of our men have re-enlisted for the Veterans Corps. They will shortly be mustered as veterans and sometime this spring will visit Wisconsin in a body." Quiner Scrapbooks, 3:4. A total of 230 members of the Ninth Wisconsin Infantry ultimately reenlisted, and companies C and K received furloughs to Wisconsin in early February. Quiner, *Military History of Wisconsin*, 544.

204. Seventeen-year-old David O. Dodd was arrested after information on the capital's defenses was found in his possession while he was returning to Camden from Little Rock. A military tribunal convicted him of spying on January 5, 1864, and sentenced him to death. He was hanged at St. Johns' College in Little Rock on January 8 and won a lasting place in Arkansas's Civil War history. Thomas A. DeBlack wrote: "Though Dodd was almost certainly guilty as charged, his youth, his refusal to implicate others, and the calm dignity with which he faced his death earned him an enduring place in Arkansas history as 'the boy martyr of the Confederacy.'" Thomas A. DeBlack, *With Fire and Sword, Arkansas, 1861–1874* (Fayetteville: University of Arkansas Press, 2003), 104–5.

In The Cane Creek (Pipe Stem Cane.)

On January 29th, our company A. received orders to get ready for an extended absence to go with a wagon train of 140 wagons, to Cane Creek to bring our mules—so run down—into a better condition, so as to be in better working order for the next summer. We took provisions for 15 days, everything else necessary, and took charge of the train. Besides ourselves there were about as many men from another regiment. We proceeded in a Southerly direction, but made only 8 miles the first day. On the third day we reached the Pine Bluff Telegraph Road, in a Southerly direction from Little Rock. Here the larger part of the train remained, but part of it went on in a different direction. The guard of the main part now consisted out of equal parts of the 27th and 33rd Iowa regiments besides ourselves.[205] On the 4th day we went through dense woods, for a long time. At last we reached a very high hill, and then saw the Arkansas River to our left. There we saw several large plantations. We stopped near the home. We saw plenty of corn and made camp, in a field under large trees. Next day we went on for about a mile, down river. Here we came into a cane field so dense that we could hardly see one step ahead of us. The cane was from two to 10 feet high. This cane is green the entire year and is excellent feed for the mules.

Here close to high timber, on the shore of the river, we found a fine place and we pitched our tents. Great Cottonwood trees stood near, and looked dangerous, because they were dead but we paid no attention to this fact. The front of our tents was toward the river and was an open place. The train was arranged in the same way and the teamsters likewise had put up their tents.

205. The Twenty-seventh Iowa Infantry mustered in at Dubuque on October 3, 1862, and participated in the Little Rock Campaign before leaving the state in late January 1864 to serve in Mississippi, Louisiana, Tennessee, and Alabama. The regiment lost 24 men killed and mortally wounded and 169 to disease. The Thirty-third Iowa Infantry mustered in at Oskaloosa on October 4, 1862, and served in most of the major Arkansas actions of 1863 and 1864 before leaving the state for service in Alabama, Louisiana, and Texas. Sixty-eight men of the Thirty-third died or were mortally wounded in action and 216 died from disease. Dyer, *Compendium*, 2:1176, 1178–79.

An Accident.

Soon we had our dinner on the fire, cooking promisingly. A strong wind was blowing. Some of us became concerned because of the dead trees hanging over us. But dinner was ready and we took it to our tents. Then a crash, a cry. A great limb of a giant tree crashed into a tent. The men jumped out but the last one was struck and killed instantly. The blood ran over his face. Friederich Rossmann[206] was dead. Another man was scratched but not seriously hurt. The dead man was washed, a coffin was made best we could and next day the corpse was sent to Little Rock, where a brother[207] was among the remaining soldiers. He was buried with soldier's honors, on the soldiers' cemetery.[208] Then all our tents were moved from under the trees to an open place.

Danger of Guerillas.

Most of our time was spent hunting. There were wild hogs-cattle-wild geese-ducks-turkey etc. The turkeys were hard to get close. Parrots were plenty.[209] Sometimes we would get a flat boat and go up, down

206. Friedrich Rossman, a native of Rhine, Germany, enlisted in Company A, Ninth Wisconsin Infantry, on September 14, 1861. His fatal accident occurred on February 1, 1864, in Pulaski County, Arkansas. *Roster of Wisconsin Volunteers*, 607.

207. Paul Rossman also enlisted in Company A, 9th Wisconsin Infantry, on September 14, 1861. A corporal, Rossman survived the war and mustered out when his term of enlistment ended on December 3, 1864. *Roster of Wisconsin Volunteers*, 607.

208. Friedrich Rossman is buried in plot 71 1368 in Little Rock National Cemetery. The Department of Veterans Affairs records his date of death as February 11, 1864. Information found at http://www.interment.net/data/us/ar/pulaski/littlenat/index.htm.

209. Flocks of Carolina parakeets were common in the bottomland forests of nineteenth-century Arkansas. The birds were about twelve inches long and had bright-green bodies with orange feathers between the bill and eyes and yellow feathers on the rest of their head and necks. Their habit of stripping orchards bare led farmers to kill them in large numbers, a practice aided by the birds' habit of not abandoning wounded members of their flock. The last documented Carolina parakeet in Arkansas was seen in 1885, the last flock was seen in Florida in 1904, and the last captive bird died in the Cincinnati Zoo in 1918. Arkansas Natural Heritage Commission, "Extinct Animals (Historic Period)," *Encyclopedia of Arkansas History & Culture*, http://www.encyclopediaofarkansas.net/encyclopedia/entry-detail.aspx?search=1&entryID=2624.

and across the river. The boat sometimes was used to bring teams across the river, and people gladly paid for this service.

There are reports going that guerilla bands want to surprise us. Strong pickets were kept, but the guerillas never came. Not even a lonely hunter was molested. The people showed great respect for the Damn Dutchman. They knew that we knew what awaited us if we fell into their hands, and what we would do if they attacked us. We remained until Febr. 12th. Sometimes we would go after corn for our mules. Otherwise they would be in the Cane fields, where they had plenty of good feed and soon were in the best of condition. On Febr. 12th a boat arrived. Another regiment came and took our places and we packed up and took the road, by land, toward Little Rock. The boat went to Pine Bluff.[210] It was night when we reached the other part of our original large train. Here we remained during the night. Next morning all went on and soon we reached the Telegraph Road and here met another company of our regiment, stationed here for protection of a Government sawmill.

After a little rest we marched and passed the mill. It was a steam-driven concern and very busy. The timber around was pine and oak, very large logs. In the evening we came to Little Rock and to our old, well known camp. In the old camp came the old routine life. The first thing of Importance was the arrival of a number of fresh recruits, who were divided into companies F. and D. These soon had to drill every day.

210. The first white settler of Pine Bluff, Joseph Bonne, built a cabin there in the fall of 1819. Ten years later, Jefferson County was established, and Pine Bluff was named the county seat in August 1832. A Confederate soldier stationed in Pine Bluff early in the war observed that "Delightful gardens, tasteful lawns, and spacious streets, give the whole place an air of comfort and elegance." By the fall of 1863, however, a Kansas cavalryman wrote that "[t]here are not a dozen tasty buildings in town, and their churches—of which there is a superabundance, are wretched affairs, almost totally destitute of beauty or inside decorations." Russell E. Bearden, "Pine Bluff (Jefferson County)," *Encyclopedia of Arkansas History & Culture*, http://www.encyclopediaofarkansas.net/encyclopedia/entry-detail.aspx?search=1&entryID=908; Christ, *Civil War Arkansas*, 1863, 226.

Next came a great general drill before the Generals Steele[211], Solomon and Rice[212] and several other Army Inspectors, on Febr. 23rd. At the Parade Grounds, near the General Hospital, we made drill in Battalion and stood in battle line.[213] Many people were lined up across the street—curiosity seekers. Two companies were called out to make drill as sharp-shooters. They were directed by signal. After these, our company A. was ordered with bayonet planted and to show attack and defense movements against infantry and cavalry. It was of great Interest to the visitors. We received much favorable commend. In the days and weeks that followed a Theater and gymnasium were erected for past-time and exercise, to keep ourselves in trim.

On March 11th order came to be ready to leave. All preparations seemed to indicate a long journey and there was much guessing about our destination. "To the Red River" it was said at last.

In was 3:00 o'clock in the afternoon when all seemed ready to depart. Soon, to our great displeasure, we saw that we were to have drill with knapsack and all belongings. Cursing and swearing brought out the disgust of the regiment. These drills are made under the mental antagonism of the soldier. It was a great fiasco. After some drill under much discontent, all returned to the camp.

211. Frederick Steele was born on January 14, 1819, in Delhi, New York, and graduated from West Point in 1843. Steele led a battalion of U.S. Regulars at Wilson's Creek, Missouri, in August 1861, and was promoted to brigadier general on January 29, 1862. After leading divisions in Arkansas and Mississippi, Steele was promoted to major general on March 17, 1863. Steele commanded the Seventh Corps and the Army of Arkansas until November 29, 1864, relieved in part because of his conciliatory policies toward secessionists. He later commanded troops operating against Mobile, Alabama, and in Texas. He died on January 12, 1868. Warner, *Generals in Blue*, 474–75; Patricia J. Palmer, *Frederick Steele: Forgotten General* (Stanford, CA: Board of Trustees of Leland Stanford Junior University, 1971), 6–9.

212. Samuel A. Rice was born on January 27, 1828, in Cattaraugus County, New York. A lawyer and politician, Rice organized and was named colonel of the Thirty-third Iowa Infantry on August 10, 1862. Rice's actions in the July 4, 1863, battle of Helena led to his promotion to brigadier general on August 4, 1863. Rice was wounded in the April 30, 1864, battle of Jenkins' Ferry, and incompetent medical care led to his death on July 6, 1864. Warner, *Generals in Blue*, 401–2.

213. The parade grounds would have been on the grounds of the U.S. Arsenal in present-day MacArthur Park.

On the 13th orders came to leave. Take oilcloth-1 woolen blanket-1 shirt-one pair of socks-the necessary sewing outfit-all in knapsack-not counting what you are wearing. All else was to remain in the tents, under care of the men not fit, or not called to go on the expedition.

From now on service was easier. We had to be ready at all times and therefore no extra drill nor service. On March 14th, at 7:00 A.M. all the troops were on the Parade Ground under command of General Solomon. Each Brigade was a line for itself. We were three Infantry Brigades, in all ten regiments. The First Brigade had four regiments, the Wis. 9th-the 27th & 33 Iowa-and the 50th Indiana.[214] The other Brigades had each three regiments. Ours, the First Brigade, was under command of General Rice, who formerly had been Governor of the state of Iowa. He was an able man and great soldier.

The third Brigade was a Division under the command of General Solomon who rode up and down the line with the other officers. When all was inspected Solomon stood in front, in the middle, and gave command "Pass in Review." The others repeated and then the entire Brigade, each company a separate line, passed before the General. Then all went homeward. Artillery and cavalry were last in review.

The Guerilla and The Great Expedition to Camden.

We now had a period of rest. On the 15th two guerillas were hanged. They kicked a long time before their guerilla spirits left their habitation. It was the harvest of their evil deeds, for they boasted that

214. It was actually the Twenty-ninth Iowa Infantry, not the Twenty-seventh, that served in Rice's First Brigade; this may have been a transcription error, as Haas is usually accurate in his recollections. *OR*, 34, part 1:658. The Fiftieth Indiana Infantry mustered in at Seymour on September 12, 1861. The regiment served in Tennessee and Mississippi before joining Steele's Little Rock Expedition in 1863, and would fight in Alabama in 1865. The Fiftieth Indiana lost 57 men killed and mortally wounded and 160 to disease. Dyer, *Compendium*, 2:1138–39.

they had murdered many Union Men.[215] We are still under marching orders and drill two hours every day to keep in trim. Today is March 22nd. Instinctively we feel that soon we will start.

On The Way to The Red River In Arkansas.

Drum and Bugle sounding we marched out. (It is the greatest expedition and most dangerous I attended. On March 23, it began and on the 3rd of May it ended.) Our knapsacks packed, as mentioned before, and gun on shoulder we marched out. After about a mile, we stopped and waited to have the other regiments come up, for we were the first regiment, in the first Brigade.

When all the regiments were out, and the road was crowded with Blue-coats signal was given to march. The Generals Solomon and Rice rode ahead. The former was in command of the entire Infantry Division and the latter of our Brigade, comprising the 9th Wisconsin, the 29th and 33rd Iowa and the 50th Indiana regiments. The latter the largest of all. We proceeded directly South until we came to the Benton Telegraph Road. We only made 10 miles and then made camp, in an open field, by a creek. The entire infantry camped on one farm. The cavalry, ahead of us, camped in timber and part of them on the next farm. Some of them covered the rear. The artillery was divided among the Infantry. We had a battery with 4 cannon, most of the other regiments had six cannon.[216]

215. The guerrillas were Jeremiah Earnest of Montgomery County and Thomas Jefferson Miller of Hempstead County, of whom a local newspaper wrote: "Their guilt of participating in the hanging of the two Osborns and Childers, on the Antoine in Clark county, in July last year was beyond controversy." *National Daily Democrat* (Little Rock), March 26, 1864. Charles Musser of the Twenty-ninth Iowa wrote to his father that "two Guerrillas were hung in front of the Penitentiary. one was a Captain by the name of Earnest. the other was a member of his company. It was proved positively that Earnest was accessory to the hanging of twenty three Union men in and around this city. Some since we came here were hung by him but a few miles from town....There are hundreds of men in this that deserve hanging as much as Earnest did, and if a man ever did need hanging, he certainly did." Barry Popchock, ed., *Soldier Boy: The Civil War Letters of Charles O. Musser, 29th Iowa* (Iowa City: University of Iowa Press, 1995), 112–13.

216. This was Captain Martin Voegele's Wisconsin Battery, which was manned by the men of Company F, Ninth Wisconsin Infantry. Edwin C. Bearss, *Steele's Retreat from Camden and the Battle of Jenkins' Ferry* (Little Rock: Pioneer Press, 1967), 168.

There was much noise and commotion during the day, but at night, when the trumpet gave the signal, quiet fell over all. Sometimes Infantry, Cavalry and Artillery signals became mixed, because all camped close together, causing much confusion and then loud laughter from many thousands of throats. When "taps" was sounded—many Drums and Bugles making a fearful noise—a gigantic laughter would close the end of the day.

March 24th.

Today, soon after breakfast the trumpet called us to assembly for marching. Soon we were going and this time the second Brigade was in the lead. It was the order that we change position, the regiment as well as the Brigade. We went on slowly and late in the afternoon came to Benton. On the North side is an abandoned Fort, for there seems to be no danger in this part of the country.[217] We entered Benton and went on down a hill to a clearing and in the bordering timber made bivouac, for we had no tents, necessity is the mother of wisdom. Rain has fallen and it is raining still. Two soldiers chum together. Out came the pocket knife. We cut two forked sticks. For up we put them into the ground, about seven feet apart. Now a pole over the stick and then the two rolls of oilcloth over the pole and the sides fastened to the ground. Now brush and leaves on the ground inside. That gives room & bed for two. From the gable end we crawl in, lie down and sleep. That is soldier's bivouac. If rain is very copious, then fence rails go below the brush, and grass over the rails. Then the water can flow below. We go in and out on all fours. In good weather the oil-cloth is put on the ground, we stretch out on it and cover with our woolen blanket. Then all is well. Over us is the great blue tent and the stars are our candles.

---

217. The fort in Benton was constructed prior to December 3, 1863, when Frederick Steele reported on potential Confederate offensive activity in Arkansas, writing, "It is reported that Kirby Smith, in a speech at Washington a short time since, said that they would take their Christmas dinner in Little Rock....We have erected some works at Benton, and the fort here [Little Rock] is progressing." OR, 53:589.

March 25th

In the morning the rain was over. We dismantled our palace. All is rolled up into the knapsack. We take our coffee and bread (the Kuckuh may call it bread)[218] but pardon—we have nothing else and in such case we only wish we had enough, but this is not so on this entire expedition. Two crackers, five inches square and one quarter inch thick, and ¼ ration bacon, two inches square and one inch thick. This in the morning, at noon and in the evening.[219] We are simply living high. This and daily marching keeps us humble. At about 10:00 A.M. the trumpets called and off we went. Through a swamp, soft with rain, roads were almost impassible. It was a long time before we came out. The first was a farm at the edge of the swamp. Gladly we jumped the fence to get out of the morass. At the house we gathered, formed lines and now proceeded on better roads. Up and down hill we went. Behind us came the Brigade Train under great difficulty and often stuck in the mud. Often the last wagon left the old camp when the front wagon began to make the camp for the next night. Soon we had to make bivouac again and slept, unless you have to be out on picket.

Rock Port.

Early in the morning we went on, through timber, and hardly saw a human habitation. It was deep, gray, sandy soil and we made slow progress. After a march of 15 miles we came to a small town Rockport—mentioned before—but did not see the town, because we camped in heavy oak timber, near the town. We remained a short time and would only be disturbed in our rest when called to our Beans or Pea-soup. Some

218. Haas is most likely referring to hardtack, the universal "bread" of the Civil War, and his statement that the "cuckoo" call it bread can be understood. Equally despised by both Union and Confederate soldiers, the unleavened flour biscuits were also known as "a castle for worms." Garrison, *Encyclopedia of Civil War Usage*, 105.

219. Andrew F. Sperry of the Thirty-third Iowa wrote: "On the evening of the second day, camping early in a good place, we drew our first rations for the trip, and learned that during the march, but half-rations would be issued." Steele's army would be troubled by hunger throughout the Camden Expedition. Gregory J. W. Urwin and Cathy Kunziger Urwin, eds., *History of the 33d Iowa Infantry Volunteer Regiment 1863–6* (Fayetteville: University of Arkansas Press, 1999), 73.

times we would have fresh meat with it. Some times noon and evening meal was all in one, because cooking is hard to do when on the march. Mostly coffee only is cooked and fortunately of that we have full rations.

March 27th.

Today, at 10:00 A.M. we marched through Rock Port and about a mile beyond we came to the Washita River. Our Pioneers had prepared a Pontoon Bridge to let our Infantry cross. Such a bridge is constructed upon air cushions about 10 feet long, made out of rubber. Air is blown into them, three sacks are fastened together and then serve in the manner of a canoe. These are anchored some distance apart and planks put upon them. Then the bridge is ready, it is wiggly but men can pass over.

After crossing and resting a little we went on across high hills After going about 8 miles we entered a deep valley, once cultivated but now lying idle. A large brook meandered through the valley. We made camp at the brookside, on a fine green meadow. The other side is high and rocky and seemingly we shall climb up in the morning. Here several guerillas were caught and shot, because they had murdered several of our cavalry.

March 28th.

We were the last Brigade to start this morning and therefore it was late when we left camp. We crossed the brook and climbed the hill. We came to a farm and after marching about seven miles farther came to the first school house. Here we made camp and prepared our evening meal. When all was about ready the order came "Ready to advance." All was turned over and soon we were on the march. After we had made about four miles we halted and made camp in an open field. The country is but thinly settled. The houses are barn-like, have two divisions and shutters instead of windows. Often there are holes in the walls only. The chimneys are built on the outside and fireplaces generally on the inside. We marched on through better and more settled country and came to a river. For some time we had to go down river to find a bridge to cross.

Then we took up the former road and direction and after some time saw trees we had never seen before, large Beech trees. After a little while we came to a deep valley and found a destroyed Powder Mill. At an earlier date it had been destroyed by our cavalry. Now we had to climb a high hill. From the top of this hill we saw a beautiful town, Archidelphia.[220] We turned to the left and made camp in the woods. Close by was a cemetery, containing some brick vaults, 4 and 5 feet high.[221]

March 29th.

Today we rested and took occasion to see the country and to hunt domesticated or other game. We really expected to get beef and hoped to find it near the Washita River, not far away. This river is navigable, at high water, but trees had been felled into it before our arrival, to hinder our coming. The people had expected us to come in boats, on the river, and had planted some cannon to greet us. There they awaited us and we were behind them in town. Their plans and strategy had failed. Our hunting trip was fruitless and we went back to camp. We had found much butchered cattle but abstained because we wanted to do our own butchering. In camp we found that some had brought flour, others beef, some even ham, and at once cooking and frying was the order of the day, in soldiers' fashion.[222]

220. William Blakeley in 1808 established a residence and blacksmith shop on the Ouachita River at a site that would become Arkadelphia by the late 1830s. The town became the Clark County seat in 1842 and would house a Confederate supply depot and ordnance works during the Civil War. S. Ray Granade, "Arkadelphia (Clark County)," *Encyclopedia of Arkansas History & Culture*, http://www.encyclopediao-farkansas.net/encyclopedia/entry-detail.aspx?search=1&entryID=848.

221. This was probably the Blakely Graveyard on South Third Street, which was closed in 1869. Some of the burials there were moved to the Maddox Cemetery when it opened in 1876, and that cemetery later became the present Rose Hill Cemetery. Holly Hope, "Rose Hill Cemetery," National Register of Historic Places nomination, Arkansas Historic Preservation Program, Little Rock, 1998.

222. Alfred Sperry wrote that the men of the Thirty-third Iowa also found food in Arkadelphia: "Very soon after breaking ranks, our men were pretty well distributed around town, seeing the sights and searching for eatables. There was little, if any foraging done. We paid for nearly all we got; and the women of the place frequently told us, 'Yur men treat us better than our own men do.' A considerable amount of good ham, cornmeal and molasses was obtained." Urwin and Urwin, *History of the 33d Iowa*, 76.

March 31st.

We are still at rest. The town has some very beautiful dwellings and many stores, and must have had good trade. Nothing doing at present. It has churches and schools as rarely found. There are about 100 dwellings. Several fine ladies are arrested because they had planted poisonous molasses openly before their homes. Several of our soldiers had taken and were dangerously sick.[223] What happened to these ladies I have not learned.

Our cavalry advance guards were driven in by a rebel band under General Marmaduke.[224] A light skirmish ensued and the rebels retired. Two rebel carriers of dispatches were caught.

April 1st

We left Archidelphia departing in a Southwestern direction, on the way to Little Washington.[225] The country is richer and more inhabited. We see find farms and plantations. A fine cotton field stood as it had ripened last summer. The cotton in part lay on the ground and in part on the plants. From the distance it looked like a snow-covered field. The slaves had deserted and the men were in the army, conscripts or volunteers. At 4:00 P.M. we came to a little village formerly Greenville,

223. Michael Zimmer also heard this rumor, writing on March 29: "I heard that 5 cavalrymen have been poisoned by molasses, they belonged to the 1st Missouri Cavalry Regiment." Macha and Wolf, *Michael Zimmer's Diary*, 187–88.

224. John Sappington Marmaduke was born on March 14, 1833, near Arrow Rock, Missouri. Perhaps the best-educated general in the Trans-Mississippi, he studied at both Harvard and Yale before graduating in the West Point class of 1857. Marmaduke advanced rapidly in the Confederate army, gaining brigadier rank on November 15, 1862. After fighting in Arkansas and Missouri, he was captured in Kansas and was imprisoned when he was promoted to major general on March 18, 1865. He died on December 28, 1887, while serving as governor of Missouri. Warner, *Generals in Gray*, 211–12.

225. The site of Washington was first settled around 1818 and was designated the county seat for Hempstead County in 1824, though the town would not be incorporated until 1830. Washington became the capital of Confederate Arkansas after the Union army occupied Little Rock on September 10, 1863. Steven Teske, "Washington (Hempstead County)," *Encyclopedia of Arkansas History & Culture*, http://www.encyclopediaofarkansas.net/encyclopedia/entry-detail.aspx?entryID=5606.

at present called Spoonville.[226] It is enclosed in the woods and not worthy of a name. A careless soldier took a shot at a deserting hog and unfortunately wounded one of our soldiers, but not dangerously.

The Little Rebel.

Six of our men rode out on patrol. Suddenly not far away—in the woods—a gun was fired and the bullet whizzed by. At the same moment we saw a little fellow re-load his gun, for another shot. To our surprise, it was a little rebel of about 13 years. What must we do? Quickly we rode up and demanded his surrender and gun. To our surprise he was in greatest anger, defending himself, striking with his gun and saying that he never would surrender to the d. Yankees. Then one of our men took his revolver and knocked him in the head. Now stunned, the youngster fell down and we brought him in as a prisoner.

The First Attack. (Apr. 2nd.)[227]

Today we marched early through well settled country. Soon we came to a new-lately built house. A man with one arm stood there, looking at us, as we marched by. We paid no attention to him, but our rear Guard did not trust him and took him along, as prisoner. He had even then set fire to the house. We had gone about a mile when at once, cannon began to roar behind us. We stopped and waited. Three of our

226. This small Clark County community has had a number of names. As Greenville, it was the Clark County seat from 1830 until Arkadelphia became the seat in 1842. A post office was established there in 1860 and named Hollywood in recognition of the many holly trees in the area. While a Mr. Witherspoon established a hotel there before the Civil War, a Spoonville post office was not established until after the war. Jacob Worthan, "Hollywood (Clark County)," *Encyclopedia of Arkansas History & Culture*, http://www.encyclopediaofarkansas.net/encyclopedia/entry-detail.aspx?search=1&entryID=7159.

227. Rice's First Brigade was guarding the Union army's wagon train when Brigadier General Joseph O. Shelby's Confederates attacked at Terre Noir Creek at noon on April 2. The Twenty-ninth Iowa, Ninth Wisconsin, Fiftieth Indiana, and Voegele's Wisconsin Battery fought off Shelby's men in a lively engagement before advancing to Okolona around 10 p.m. OR, 34, part 1:684–85.

regiments were behind us and these were attacked and almost captured. But with assistance of the Second Regiment, the enemy was driven back with heavy losses. But like little dogs they would attack again when our men would take up the march, following the train. The rebel General had sworn that before sundown he would capture the train of the Yankees at any cost and now tried anything possible. We marched on despite the roaring of cannon behind us.

Not very long and cannon began to roar ahead of us.[228] Now we were attacked from front and rear. There is little fun in such a position. Soon we came to a road leading off to our left, which we took. Here the second Battalion[229] of our Regiment was ordered to remain and to be ready to assist the others. We—the First Battalion[230]— marched on to follow our train. We had not gone far into the timber, when we were ordered to stop and did a little while. The roar of guns continued. One queer old Major with us made the remark: "Lucky dogs we are, like always that we are not allowed to have a hand in this hoggish deal." But he had lauded the day before the evening. After a little while we received orders to speedily come back to the aid of our hard pressed men, who kept up a strong musket fire and at our arrival just began to push back the rebels. The dry leaves between us and the enemy were on fire and the dense smoke hid the rebels so that they could not be seen, when very near to us. Very soon we were in battle array in smoke, fire of the rebels and the burning leaves. Before we came very close, the cannon balls roared over our heads, high up in the trees and then fell down, some on our heads. Soon the rebels retired and we were ordered to follow our train. We had hardly taken the road and the rebels fired again from behind. We had to follow our train as tirailleurs,[231] behind the column of troops and jump from tree to tree, as the bullets of the rebels whizzed around us. The

228. Voegele reported firing 138 rounds during the fighting at Terre Noir Creek. *OR*, 34, part 1:704.

229. This consisted of companies B, E, G, and H. *OR*, 34, part 1:703.

230. This consisted of companies A, D, and I. *OR*, 34, part 1:703.

231. Tirailleurs were skirmishers.

rebels came closer and soon we were ordered to form battle line, to receive them. This done we could jump behind our line and arrange ourselves with them. Now our cannons began to roar against those of the enemy and soon theirs gave way. By this time, evening shadows were falling. The rebels could no longer see us and ceased their useless pressure. They fell back. We marched on and during the night came to the town Oenelone.[232] Here, the next night we slept on cotton, turned out of the large bales.

The man with the one arm, who had set the new house on fire when we had passed, had thereby given signal to the rebels that the last of us had passed. They could now attack from our rear and would not have yankees behind them. This one-armed fellow will surely receive judgment as a spy. Our regiment lost 14 men and the others had similar losses.[233] The rebels lost more, because they came so close that they could almost take us by the hair and would call, "Halt, halt you are our prisoner." Ours would not surrender but turn and fire into the crowd of rebels. One of our Captains heard the word "Halt" and thought it was given by our Major—swore violently, calling angrily: "What halt? How can I halt here? Donner Wetter-forward, march. Here let the devil halt, when the rebels almost ride over us." Some of ours were cut off but were not in the mood to be made prisoners. They hid in the timber till night. In the dark they heard footsteps, and from talk learned that they were rebels on picket duty. They heard that orders were given for keenest watch and to shoot any one who would not stand on call to surrender. Stealthily, on all fours, they crawled over to our line. They had to make a long crawl around the enemy picket line and had nothing to eat. The 29th Iowa regiment had lost 30 men in the

232. A post office was established at Okolona in southwestern Clark County in 1858, and the town boasted several general stores by the time Steele's army arrived there in 1864. David Sesser, "Okolona (Clark County)," *Encyclopedia of Arkansas History & Culture*, http://www.encyclopediaofarkansas.net/encyclopedia/entry-detail.aspx?search=1&entryID=7027.

233. The Ninth Wisconsin suffered one man wounded and 11 missing, the Fiftieth Indiana four men killed, 12 wounded and four missing, and Voegele's Battery had one man wounded on April 2. OR, 34, part 1:692.

first attack.[234] Despite continual fight, in front and rear, we made 15 miles that day.[235]

Here close to our camp near the house was a large pile of ashes. Some of our men did not trust that pile, inspected and found in it a barrel full of the finest of ham. All was divided under the greatest merriment. The lady of the house came and gave a sharp tongue lashing to the keen scented Yankees, who spy everything. Laughter and derision was all she received.

April 3rd.

We marched forward but the third Brigade was expected to return to aid the cavalry at Little Washington where they could not get the mastery over the rebels. More men were needed to turn the tide.

Hardly had we left when the rebels were at it again and killed several in the camp. Some of ours returned to give them a morning greeting. The rebels however preferred not to come close enough for a

234. The Twenty-ninth Iowa lost four men killed, 17 wounded, and four missing in the fight at Terre Noir Creek. OR, 34, part 1:692.

235. Michael Zimmer's entry for April 3 agrees with that of Haas and offers more details: "The 2nd. We were attacked by the rebels today, and indeed from three sides. In the rear there was the first attack by General Marmaduke with his troops. The 50th Indiana Regiment was on a rear guard, apart from two pieces of artillery from our battery which were commanded by Captain Vogele [sic] from our regiment, Company F. The battery consists of 4 pieces and belongs to our regiment....We had to guard the train, namely Companies E, G, H, and B of our regiment. Companies A, I, and D were up ahead between the wagons. The 50th Indiana Regiment and the two pieces of artillery were under fire for about 1 ½ hours. Immediately we stopped, let the 50th Regiment and the two pieces artillery pass us and took up the fight against the enemy, that is the 4 above mentioned companies and the two pieces of artillery we had with us. The firing got more and more intense, but the 4 companies resisted and fought like lions. Our brigadier was always with us, even in the heaviest hail of bullets and shouted: Bully for the Ninth, which really encouraged us, but in the end they were too strong for our 4 companies. General Reis made the other 3 companies of our regiment join us to reinforce us, but they withstood us till night. We had 23 dead and many wounded men, I could not find out anything about losses of the enemy....We did 16 miles with all that, even though they pestered us on three sides, but were tired and exhausted when we arrived in our camp." Macha and Wolf, Michael Zimmer's Diary, 188–89.

handshake.[236] Then we marched again up and down hill until we reached the Little Missouri River, where we made camp in a wild, swampy-like timber. There had been heavy rains and we had to cut green branches of the Wintergreen trees to avoid sleeping in the mud. These trees have small prickly branches and are green the entire year. Vines—climbers—make it impossible to go forward during the night. We gathered corn and butchered cattle. The meat was fried in pans or roasted on sticks over the fire.

The Battle (April 4th)[237]

Early in the morning we heard the speech of cannon, at our front. The 36th Iowa and 43rd Illinois had crossed the river the day before and made camp.[238] Here the rebels attacked them. When our men went to meet them the rebels retired and ours after them until they perceived that the rebels fell back only to have other of their forces cut them off. Then ours retired and the rebels again attacked and drove them to the

236. Shelby's Confederates attacked the Union rearguard at Okolona at 9 a.m. on April 3, and a sharp skirmish, augmented by a violent thunderstorm that pelted the combatants with hail, lasted for several hours before Shelby withdrew. Union losses were three killed and seven wounded, while Shelby's were not reported. Mark Christ, "Skirmishes at Okolona," *Encyclopedia of Arkansas History & Culture*, http://www.en-cyclopediaofarkansas.net/encyclopedia/entry-detail.aspx?search=1&entryID=4442.

237. Advance elements of Steele's army crossed the Little Missouri River on April 3 and skirmished with Confederate cavalry. Marmaduke met a more concentrated effort to cross on April 4 with twelve hundred Rebel horsemen. After five hours of sometimes intense combat, Marmaduke withdrew his forces sixteen miles to Prairie D'Ane. Union forces suffered 26 wounded, while Confederate casualties were 29 killed, wounded, and missing in the engagement at Elkin's Ferry. Daniel Sutherland, "1864: 'A Strange, Wild Time,'" in *Rugged and Sublime: The Civil War in Arkansas*, ed. Mark K. Christ (Fayetteville: University of Arkansas Press, 1994), 111–12.

238. The Thirty-sixth Iowa Infantry Regiment was organized at Keokuk and mustered in on October 4, 1862. With the exception of one excursion into Mississippi, the regiment saw all of its service in Arkansas. It mustered out on August 24, 1865, after losing 65 men killed or mortally wounded and 238 from disease. The Forty-third Illinois was mustered in at Camp Butler, Illinois, on October 12, 1861, and was involved in heavy action in Tennessee and Mississippi before transferring to Arkansas after the fall of Vicksburg in 1863. The Forty-third mustered out at Camp Butler on December 14, 1865, recording 83 men killed or mortally wounded and 163 dead from disease. Dyer, *Compendium*, 2:1065, 1179–80.

bank of the river. We now plainly heard heavy musket firing mingled with the roar of cannon. By this time the 29th Iowa had crossed the river to aid them and now we and our battery went over in the midst of a rain of rebel bullets. Cannon now roared from both sides. When we followed the roar of our cannon, our brave General Rice met us and gave welcome in the words "We will send these traitors to hell before we leave this place." But we were stunned when we saw blood run down both sides of his face and saw pain in his features. When we expressed our sympathy he only said: "It is a pity because of my cap because it cost me $5.00 and it is entirely torn." A piece of shell had torn the cap and wounded him in the head. It came close to taking his life.[239] He put us in position on the right side of the road, where we were close to a creek; formed for attack. The rebs saw that there was nothing to gain and withdrew. We kept our position and threw up breastworks from old logs and remained, gun in hand.

The Disturbed Peace.

We remained until about 4:00 p.m. Then we were ordered to return to our former position. Here we had our noon and evening meal—both in one—and rested after the day's troubles. The brave conduct of our General gave him the confidence of all the soldiers. We lost 13 men, captured one Howitzer and made one Major of Marmaduke's staff our prisoner,[240] who admitted that the Bluejackets were hardier than they had expected. They had expected to capture men and cannon, but had failed.

---

239. Captain Edward Ruegger of Company E, Ninth Wisconsin Infantry, wrote: "Our Brigadier General Rice was badly wounded on the head, but could not be induced to leave the battlefield, although blood ran over his face all the time." Edward Ruegger, "Five Weeks of My Army Life," Wisconsin Historical Society Library and Archives, Madison, Wisconsin, 2.

240. The captured officer was not a major, but Lieutenant Wiley B. Fackler, an aide-de-camp to Marmaduke taken by the Thirty-sixth Iowa Infantry. Banasik, *Reluctant Cannoneer*, 227n.

April 5th.

We were not molested today in any way but learned that the Brigade of Col. Engelmann, which had returned from Okelone, was in battle with the rebels at the village Washington, where our cavalry had trouble with rebs at an earlier date.[241]

April 6th.

Today our entire force crossed the river. The cavalry was ahead of us and the regiment followed next. We now saw the effect of our artillery. Trees were shattered and torn. Soon we heard skirmish firing at our front. Our cavalry went forward on both flanks and pressed the rebels out of their barricades, behind which they had expected to surprise us. The bad roads made progress difficult for our train, despite the greatest efforts of our Pioneers to improve the roads.

Water became very scarce and soon we had to camp, on a small farm, in the timber.[242] On this farm we saw many graves. Here 24 rebels had been buried. Here many slaves deserted and came to us, with all their belongings and rejoiced in their liberty.

Rest and Corn.

April 7th. Today we are resting, awaiting our forces from Fort Smith, to augment our forces before we go on. These are under com-

241. Colonel Adolph Engelmann, commanding the Third Brigade, reported sending small cavalry patrols toward Washington and a nearby mill, but no combat activity on April 5. OR, 34, part 1:721. Engelmann was born on February 11, 1825, at Imsbach, Bavaria, and was the colonel of the Forty-third Illinois Infantry Regiment. He would receive a brevet promotion to brigadier general of volunteers on March 13, 1865, for "faithful and meritorious services." He died on October 5, 1890, at Shiloh, Illinois. Roger D. Hunt and Jack R. Brown, *Brevet Brigadiers in Blue* (Gaithersburg, MD: Olde Soldier Books, 1990), 194.

242. Elements of Steele's army camped on the farm of the Widow Cornelius to await Thayer's Frontier Division. OR, 34, part 1:675.

mand of General Jaeger.[243] We are under the Blue Dome and upon dry leaves. Our time is spent in grinding corn to replenish our rations by 50%. The grinding is done on a large coffee mill and then large corn-cakes are made. These taste well when rations are short. But even the corn we have to swipe, for there is not enough for the multitude of men and mules.

Train and Troops from Fort Smith.

April 8th. With other regiments—about 700 cavalry and ten can-non—we marched about 4 miles until we came to a cross-road to watch against attack of rebels against a large provision train, which had been sent out. After some time the train arrived and all returned. The rebels no doubt knew the trap we had set and did not come to attack the fine train of 70 wagons.

April 9th We are still at rest. Some rebels molested our pickets but were easily driven off. Toward evening the troops of General Jaeger, to augment our forces, arrived. They consist of four cavalry and six Infantry regiments, among them two regiments of colored soldiers. They have two full Batteries, of six cannon each, and six Howitzers with the cavalry.[244] These regiments, on the march, had been very short on provisions, and a full train was sent to meet them. They received no more than we did

243. John Milton Thayer was born on January 24, 1820, in Bellingham, Massachusetts. A lawyer, he moved to the Nebraska Territory in 1854, and gained a positive reputation as an Indian fighter as head of the territorial militia. When the Civil War began, he was colonel of the First Nebraska Infantry, was promoted to brigadier general on March 13, 1863, and commanded a division at Vicksburg. Thayer took command of the District of the Frontier, based in Fort Smith, on February 22, 1864. Though demoted to a minor command just over a year later, he received a brevet promotion to major general before resigning his commission on July 19, 1865. He became one of Nebraska's first U.S. senators after it gained statehood, served as Wyoming Territory's governor, and served a term as governor of Nebraska. He died on March 19, 1906. Warner, *Generals in Blue*, 499–500.

244. Thayer's Frontier Division of about thirty-six hundred men consisted of the First and Second Arkansas, Eighteenth Iowa, Twelfth Kansas, and First and Second Kansas Colored infantry regiments; the Second, Sixth, and Fourteenth Kansas cavalry regiments; and the First Arkansas and Second Indiana artillery batteries. *OR*, 34, part 1:658.

because we too were short. The Negro regiments were greeted with great enthusiasm, and they proved themselves good soldiers.[245]

April 10th. We were to make an early start but it was afternoon before all were ready. We marched several miles, unmolested, until we came to a prairie. Then we heard rumbling of cannon at our front. Soon it grew into strong turbulence. We hurried on and behind the cannon battle line was formed. Before us, on the hill, cannon hurried from one place to another, under a hail of enemy artillery. Many shells exploded near us but none did us any harm.

Before us, on a hill, we saw the enemy artillery. Our artillery was sent through the woods, right and left, and when they opened fire, the rebels fled across the prairie, but halted again at the edge of a timber line. Our Batteries, by this time, had taken position on a hill and poured their fire into the new position of the rebels, who answered in an inferior way. Night came on. We followed our artillery upon the prairie and remained in battle line. No campfire was made, no coffee, nothing to eat nor to drink.

Myself and others had just been ordered out on watch and were marching to headquarters when enemy cannon balls fell close to us and covered us with dirt. Other balls came farther or closer and often we had to lie down on the ground to escape being hit by fractions of shells. We proceeded farther into the prairie and then dodged into the grass,

245. The First Kansas Colored Infantry was recruited in October 1862 and saw action at Island Mound, Missouri, on October 27, 1862—the first black troops in combat during the Civil War—before their official muster at Fort Scott on January 13, 1863. The First Kansas served in Kansas, Missouri, Arkansas, and the Indian Territory before their designation as the Seventy-ninth U.S. Colored Troops on December 13, 1864. The Seventy-ninth would serve out the rest of the war in Arkansas before mustering out at Pine Bluff on October 1, 1865, and discharged at Fort Leavenworth, Kansas, on October 30, 1865. The regiment lost 188 men killed and mortally wounded and 166 to disease. Dyer, *Compendium*, 2:1186–87, 1735. The Second Kansas Colored Infantry was organized at Fort Scott and Fort Leavenworth between August 11 and October 17, 1863. The regiment served in Kansas and Arkansas before being designated the Eighty-third U.S. Colored Troops on December 13, 1864. The Eighty-third served the rest of the war in Arkansas, mustered out at Camden on October 9, 1865, and was discharged at Leavenworth, Kansas, on November 27, 1865. The regiment lost 34 men killed and mortally wounded and 211 to disease. Dyer, *Compendium*, 2:1187, 1736.

on watch duty. From here we could distinctly see the flash of the enemy's guns and then hear the explosions of the shells behind us.

By this time our artillery had become impatient. A full battery now let loose against the rebels. These seemed to hesitate a little while but soon began again. Our Batteries answered in same way but every time from a changed position. The entire regiment kept on the move and therefore had no more rest than we had on picket duty.—After the cannon had spoken, from both sides for some time, the muskets began to rattle.

It grew in intensity and soon we saw the glitter of enemy bayonets before us and bullets, bee-like, hum around us. We were not slow to answer. Then, for a while, all became quiet. Soon, from our right wing the artillery came in and now again mixed with the rattle of muskets. This battery of our right wing the enemy had expected to capture. But our infantry—ahead of the cannon, in the grass—spoiled their plan.

This infantry gave them such hot reception that they did not try a second attack. One of our men, rising too high out of the grass, was killed by our own artillery, behind us. This went on up to midnight. It was cold. We all shivered. Thirty rebel pickets were surprised and such who resisted were shot. The majority of them surrendered. Our long train stood in line, a mile behind us, and Jaeger's division guarded the same. The prairie is called "De Ann Prairie," is quite long and about a mile wide. On the edge of the prairie are several farms. The cattle here have free range. On our side is considerable brush. We lost several men in dead and wounded.[246]

---

246. Michael Zimmer wrote of the action on April 10: "About 3 o'clock we attacked them and onwards we went under a permanent rumble of gunfire. We proceeded slowly, but steadily, we drove them back 3 miles, then formed a trailer line and the rest of our troops fell in into battle line. Thus everything went on under a terrible rumble of gunfire till night, at 11 o'clock they tried to storm one of our batteries several times, but every time they were fought back and suffered heavy losses. The battlefield was called Prairie de Ann." Macha and Wolf, *Michael Zimmer's Diary*, 190. Rice's brigade was on the left of Salomon's Third Division as they attacked on the first day of fighting at Prairie D'Ane, which is located near the present-day city of Prescott. (Note: There are several spellings of this battle; Prairie D'Ane is preferred by the National Park Service.) The division would lose three killed and fourteen wounded during the fighting on the prairie. *OR*, 34, part 1:687–88.

April 11th. Today, before sunrise, everybody is up and alert, and wants to see what is going on. About two miles ahead of us, over the prairie we see smoke from the camp of the enemy, and about 1/4 mile from us we see their pickets—a line across the entire prairie. One rebel on a white horse is riding along the line from one picket to the other. It is beautiful sunshine now and we feel comfortable and have more life in us.

Soon we were ordered into battle line. We, the first Brigade, on the right wing, of the first line—for there were three lines. The third line was the cavalry. When all was in order we went forward, across the prairie. We went in columns and the batteries between us. The banners fluttered in the wind. It was a stirring vision.

We came close to the timber, on the opposite side of the prairie. Here halt was made and the cannon began to growl. The rebels too began to throw their bombs and shells. But they did not seem to hit. One of our batteries pounded the rebels before and behind a home. Here we remained, lying in the grass until darkness fell upon us. Sharpshooters kept up the fire. From shelter, often sharp epithets were thrown across. The rebels offered us coffee and we them cauer kraut—if they come and get it. Distance between us was not great. Our general rode about and tried to locate and measure the enemy. When night came we returned to the position of the previous night. The enemy did not trouble us that night because they did not know our location. All we had to eat was half a ration of crackers. Fire was not allowed.[247]

247. Andrew Sperry of the Thirty-third Iowa in Rice's brigade wrote of April 11: "At 2:25 in the afternoon, a forward movement commenced. The whole of our little army was drawn up in battle array, in such a disposition that it looked even to ourselves like a large force, and to the rebels in our front, must have seemed an utterly over-whelming array of infantry, cavalry and artillery....Certainly it was to us, and must have been more to them, a magnificent spectacle. The vast prairie, with its beautiful diversity of groves and undulations, was just the ground for such a display; and we can not easily forget the enthusiasm awakened by the martial scene." Urwin and Urwin, *History of the 33d Iowa*, 83. Despite the martial display, no attack followed and the Union troops returned to their lines that evening.

To The Attack.

April 12. Nothing warm to drink in the morning. We received water but it was dirty white. At 6:00 a.m. all was in motion. Our leaders were everywhere. We felt that today a decision was to come. Our advance guards started and we after them. Quickly we crossed prairie but turned more to the right than yesterday. The right wing turned toward the farm house. There, yesterday, the rebels stood in the timber. Our left wing advanced slowly, but kept in line. The first battery took position and bombarded the home. We had, by this time, marched upon the field behind the house and torn down the fences. Here we found the enemy had erected breastworks and we expected hard fight. All our forces advanced—artillery and cavalry. But behold the enemy was gone. Their breastworks we found empty. Now we saw. We had flanked them and spoiled their plans. The breastworks were useless and a battle in the open they would not risk. We had offered battle yesterday and would have forced it today. They did not accept. It was fortunate that our leaders had suspected their plan. We saw the danger and death-trap and rejoiced.[248]

The Army.

We made pursuit about 1/2 mile on the little Washington Road, and then returned, for our aim was in the opposite direction. When we returned to the prairie nothing but blue-jackets could be seen, their

---

248. The Confederate army pulled back to within eight miles of Washington during the night of April 11–12, and Steele decided to stop moving toward Shreveport and instead seek supplies in Camden for his starving army. Sutherland, "1864: A Strange, Wild Time," 113–14. With the movement from Prairie D'Ane, Steele lost tactical initiative. As historian Michael Forsyth observed, "It must be noted that the point at which Steele turned east represents the zenith of Federal fortunes in the Camden Expedition. From Prairie D'Ane onward, the entire Federal effort was a retrograde operation punctuated by unmitigated disasters to Union arms that threatened to outright destruction of the VII Corps." Michael J. Forsyth, *The Camden Expedition of 1864 and the Opportunity Lost by the Confederacy to Change the Civil War* (Jefferson, NC: McFarland and Co., 2003), 98.

bayonets glittering in the sunlight. One column stood behind the other. The banners were waving in the breeze. It was a beautiful sight, full of life and joy.

We marched on over the prairie, for we were again to take the lead. All fell in behind us. Some time after, when marching, we had a perspective over a wooded valley, and saw on the prairie we had left about two miles distant, the gigantic, snake-like form of our large train, covered with white tarpaulin, climbing up the hill and moving in same direction with us. As far as the eye could reach, wagon after wagon and six mules to each. Between them, here and there a troop of soldiers, for protection. These off and on would collect cattle and drive them along.

By and by we came into timber and found a hospital full of wounded rebels wounded by us, in the late battle. After a march of about six miles, camp was made, in the woods. Dry leaves were gathered for bedding. Fresh beef now was plentiful, and once again we could satisfy our hunger. Cattle often were killed with fence rails.

Bad Roads

After good rest and meat diet, late in the morning, our journey was taken up again. Our wagons—now ahead of us—could proceed but slowly and often we had to halt. One train with the respective brigade was ahead of us. The troops under General Jaeger were the Rear Guard. Roads became so miserable that the way had to be paved with fence rails or logs. The Pioneers worked hard but progress was very slow. It was a strange sight to see a whole regiment and each man have a fencerail on his shoulder, besides his gun.

We had not gone very far when the expected roar of cannon began again, in our rear. "Our Rear Guard is attacked" it went from mouth to mouth. The enemy did attack but our Negro regiments fell upon them with bayonets and soon drove them back. They were pursued across the former prairie battle ground and suffered heavy losses. In this fight the first Negro Regiment lost their Major. Our side lost 20 men and the enemy lost about 100.[249] Then, soon we came out of the swamp, upon a hill. It was almost night and we made camp. The larger part of our train was still in the mud.

Provision Expedition.

Apr. 14. In the morning, at 4:00 o'clock our company with four others were ordered out with empty provision train. We started and soon were in a miserable swamp again. We had great trouble in getting the empty train through. Fortunately this swamp was not very wide. Soon we came to better road. Our train divided and went out in different directions. Myself with others turned to the right of the road. Soon we came to a farm and filled our wagons with corn from a barn and then paid a visit to the smoke house and helped ourselves. From the garden fine onion went with us. We went back the same road, others joined and soon all were in.

Before long, orders came to get ready for a speedy departure the coming night. Everything except our oilcloth was left behind. We departed and through deep sand, up and down hill, night came and we came in touch with rebel pickets. We made camp on a large farm. Fence rails and dry grass made good camp fire.

249. Realizing that Steele's goal was not Washington, Confederate Major General Sterling Price ordered his cavalry to pursue the Union army. They caught up with Steele's rear-guard, Thayer's Frontier Division, at the village of Moscow, but withdrew after a heated action that cost Thayer seven dead and 31 wounded; Confederate losses were not reported. Frank Arey, "Action at Moscow," *Encyclopedia of Arkansas History & Culture*, http://www.encyclopediaofarkansas.net/encyclopedia/entry-detail.aspx?search=1&entryID=2513. Major Richard W. Ward of the First Kansas Colored Infantry was not lost in this battle. Ward, who had been promoted to major on May 2, 1863, after serving as captain of Company A, First Kansas Colored, would be promoted to lieutenant colonel of the regiment on April 22, 1865, and would muster out with the regiment on October 1, 1865. *Report of the Adjutant General of the State of Kansas, 1861–65* (Topeka: Kansas State Printing Company, 1896), 1:574.

Artillery Duel.

April 15. Early we started. Two regiments were ahead and the 30th Indiana[250] behind us. As generally, the cavalry, with Howitzers, was ahead of all. We had gone about 4 miles when the Howitzers at our front began to bark. We learned that our advance guard had scared up a rebel nest. Soon we came to the Little Washington Road. Here we found many earmarks of nearness of rebels. We were just climbing up a hill, when our Howitzers again lifted up their voices. Soon the large cannon joined in the song. We were ordered into battle line and marched into brush, behind the large cannon, which in great haste spat shells against the rebels. We marched upward. Enemy shells shrieked and exploded about us. Dirt rained about us, mingled with steel and howling sounds in the air. We tried to protect ourselves behind trees and in any way possible. From here we could see the work of our artillery, how they hurried in loading, firing and re-setting their guns. Shells shrieked and exploded between us and our artillery, throwing up dirt into the air and others tore down trees. It was a spectacle of Hell let loose.

When our artillerists saw the flash of the enemy's guns, they quickly fell upon the ground. The shell being past they hurriedly jumped up and fired. The rebels stood about half a mile away, likewise in timber. This great artillery duel lasted about two hours with unabated fury and then ended in flight of the rebels. They lost one cannon which was demolished and hidden under leaves. One of our men was struck by a piece of shell and died later.[251] Several others of the regiment were killed and wounded—and so were some of our artillery. We wondered that not many more had been killed. The loss of the enemy never became known to us. Dead horses we saw lying about. After burial we speedily

250. Actually the Fiftieth Indiana.

251. This was Joseph Klohe of Company A, Ninth Wisconsin Infantry. Klohe, of Herman, Wisconsin, enlisted on September 17, 1861, and would die in Camden on April 17, 1864, of the wound suffered on April 15. *Roster of Wisconsin Volunteers*, 607.

advanced, but the rebels had escaped. We took up our journey. Company A. was sent out as Advance Guard.[252]

We went through fields and woods, on both sides of the road, and later were relieved by cavalry. Sometimes we came to homes and barns which had contained corn, but had been burned by the rebels to prevent falling into our hands. As Advance guard we came to Camden, where we rested, waiting to let the army come up. At sinking of night we marched into town, which the rebels had left about two hours before.[253]

We camped by the first Fort upon a hill.[254] All the trees around had been cut. From here, the rebels had expected to pour their fire upon us. Most of the citizens, except a few whites and negroes, had fled when they heard the roar of the cannon about 15 miles away. This morning we had marched 18 miles.

Camden.

April 16th. The city Camden is scattered over much ground, and has many stores and Warehouses. It has fine buildings and a

252. Rice's First Brigade had the advance position on the march into Camden and engaged in what he described as a "brisk skirmish with three brigades of rebel cavalry." He reported four men killed and fifteen wounded in the advance from Prairie D'Ane to Camden. *OR*, 34, part 1:695, 699. Andrew Sperry of the Thirty-third Iowa noted, "The skirmishing in front was so incessant that a ten-minute's silence, as once in a while occurred, seemed more noticeable and significant than the accustomed popping of the musketry." Urwin and Urwin, *History of the 33d Iowa*, 87.

253. The historian of the First Iowa Cavalry described Camden as "a large, well built town, doing quite and extensive business, and was a large depot of supplies for the rebel army. During a high stage of water the river is navigable to this place and the Red river steamboats are frequently seen here." A. F. Sperry of the Thirty-third Iowa Infantry wrote of Camden: "The neat white houses, and the general air of the place rather pleased us; and there seemed to be a lurking impression that we would stay there a while." Sperry reported that they entered Camden at about 6:30 p.m. Lothrop, *History of the First Regiment Iowa Cavalry*, 158; Urwin and Urwin, *History of the 33d Iowa*, 88.

254. The Confederate army constructed a series of five earthen redoubts on high ground surrounding Camden between January and March 1864. Steele's army would add trenches between the fortifications during its stay in Camden. William L. Shea, "The Camden Fortifications," *Arkansas Historical Quarterly* 41 (Winter 1982): 319–25.

Courthouse.[255] Its position is on the Wichita River. The river is navigable and many steamboats come and go. One large warehouse, filled
with provisions, the rebels had burned. About noon we went to the
East side and camped close to the river. Softly and warm, now we rested
on bales of cotton. A Pontoon Bridge was built across the river to let
our provision train come over, which came from Pine Bluff.

April 17th. Last night about 12:00 o'clock we were aroused from
our cotton beds. A steamboat arrived and we did not know whether
they were friends or enemies. Gun in hand we sneaked near and then
saw the stars and stripes on the steamer. Our cavalry had captured the
ship loaded with corn from the rebels.[256] At 11:00 o'clock we, and company B., were ordered across the river, after provisions. After a march
of about 8 miles we came to a large farm. With the aid of negroes we
found bacon and ham, plenty of it hidden under cotton plus molasses
and lard. The garden lost onions and the hennery its chickens. The
slaves greeted us with joy. We were the first Yankees they saw. We departed in peace.

255. Camden became a prominent trade center on the Ouachita River and in
1844 was incorporated as the county seat of Ouachita County. The brick courthouse
Haas mentions was constructed in 1858, replacing an earlier structure that burned. It,
too, would burn in December 1875. When the Civil War started, Camden was the sec-
ond-largest city in Arkansas, with more than 2,000 residents. J. E. Gaughan, "Historic
Camden," *Arkansas Historical Quarterly* 20 (Autumn 1961): 246, 249.

256. The vessel was the *Homer*, a 194-ton sidewheel packet built for $30,000 in
Parkersburg, Virginia (now West Virginia), in 1959. A detachment of the First Iowa
and Third Missouri Cavalry regiments captured it, and Lieutenant J. T. Foster of
Company B, First Iowa, a former Mississippi River steamboat pilot, sailed it to
Camden, where the 3,000 to 5,000 bushels of corn aboard were welcomed by the
hungry Yankee troops. The Federals apparently scuttled it when they left Camden,
and the Confederates would salvage materials from its superstructure to build a bridge
across the Ouachita to pursue Steele's fleeing army. Mark K. Christ, "The Homer
(Shipwreck)," National Register of Historic Places nomination, Arkansas Historic
Preservation Program, Little Rock, 2002. Michael Zimmer noted that the *Homer's*
arrival caused quite a stir: "After two hours sleep the call woke us that the enemy
was approaching with his fleet. We lined up at the river and after standing for half
an hour and waiting to receive the enemy, we got news that it was only a steamboat
which our cavalry had taken from the enemy 18 miles away." Macha and Wolf,
Michael Zimmer's Diary, 192.

April 18th. Today at 11:00 o'clock, we heard heavy cannonade in the direction from which we had come. It told us that our provision train was attacked. The train had 700 negroes and at least two cannon as guard. It contained 153 wagons. The rebels had attacked in superior force. The negroes fought bravely, even with bayonets, but had been overcome and scattered. According to rebel deserters about 100 dead and 1300 wounded rebels were left on the battlefield. The rebels captured everything, except some who fled and came back to us. Our wounded were brought in.[257]

April 20th. Today, the long looked for provision train from Pine Bluff arrived. Another empty train was sent out. We are building forts to protect our bridge.[258]

April 21. Still building protection. Negroes and rebels are coming over to us every day.

April 23. Because of rebel activities we are quartered upon a high hill on the South side of town and one of the three forts, near the hill, is occupied by our forces.[259] Later we learned that while the rebels kept

257. Confederate troops attacked a Union foraging expedition at Poison Spring on April 18 as it returned to Camden after seizing corn and plunder west of the city. After a desperate battle, the Federal column dissolved and Confederate soldiers roamed the field killing wounded and surrendered troops of the First Kansas Colored Infantry Regiment, many of whom were former slaves from Arkansas, Missouri, and the Indian Territory. Union casualties totaled 301, from which the First Kansas suffered 117 killed and 65 wounded. At least 125 white Yankees were taken prisoner. Confederate casualties numbered around 145. Gregory J. W. Urwin, "Poison Spring and Jenkins' Ferry: Racial Atrocities during the Camden Expedition," in *"All Cut to Pieces and Gone to Hell": The Civil War, Race Relations, and the Battle of Poison Spring*, ed. Mark K. Christ (Little Rock: August House/Butler Center, 2003), 110–26. Poison Spring was shocking to the Federal troops, as Michael Zimmer observed on April 19: "Today I heard the truth about yesterday's affair: oh, it was obviously a horrible slaughter….A Kansas Black Regiment is said to have been treated terribly by the rebels. They were among the crew and fought bravely. I deeply regret our losses and hope that our generals will be more careful in the future." Macha and Wolf, *Michael Zimmer's Diary*, 193.

258. Michael Zimmer wrote on April 20: "Today our company had to build fortifications on the Washita River, our company had to guard the bridge that has been built across the river." Macha and Wolf, *Michael Zimmer's Diary*, 193.

259. This was Redoubt E, which covered the Bradley Ferry Road south of Camden. It survives today in Camden's Fort Southerland Park. Shea, "The Camden Fortifications," 321.

our attention here, other of their forces attacked and captured our empty train. The whole train, a whole Brigade of infantry and a battery fell into their hands.[260] (The rebels continually molested our pickets.) Our regiment was sent out. Soon several shells silenced them & here quiet set in for the night.

April 26. Today almost every man was on picket duty, near the high hill or along the river. Toward evening instructions came to be ready to leave at a moment's notice, because of danger of being surrounded by rebels, who had received strong re-enforcements.[261] We were out of provisions because the rebels had captured everything. Other intelligence brought told that the Rebel General Kirby Smith came up from the Red River and thought to crush us after he had defeated the miserable General Banks, who now fled.[262] Banks' army had been strong, our little force he expected to crush and thereafter to take Little Rock. It was 2:00 o'clock at night when we left our watch and without noise marched through town. Then we crossed the Pontoon Bridge and made camp some distance away. When all had crossed the bridge it was taken up. When day came we marched mostly in high woods and little inhabited country. We marched 18 miles.

260. The action at Marks' Mills actually occurred on April 25, 1864. A Confederate cavalry force attacked a Union wagon train and, after a violent and confusing battle, caused around 1,500 Federal casualties, most of which were captured. The Confederates suffered only 293 killed, wounded, and missing at Marks' Mills. After the disaster, Steele decided to abandon Camden and retreat to Little Rock. Sutherland, "1864: A Strange, Wild Time," 118–19.

261. Lieutenant General Edmund Kirby Smith diverted three infantry divisions from action against Nathaniel Banks' Union army on the Red River and ordered them north on April 23 in hopes of destroying Steele's force at Camden. Bearss, *Steele's Retreat from Camden*, 92.

262. Nathaniel Prentiss Banks was born January 13, 1816, in Waltham, Massachusetts, and was serving as that state's governor when Abraham Lincoln appointed him as a major general of volunteers in 1861. His service in Virginia was disastrous and after the failure of the Red River Campaign in 1864, he was replaced as head of that army. After the war, he served six terms in Congress and nine years as a U.S. marshal before dying on September 1, 1894. Warner, *Generals in Blue*, 17–18.

April 28. Our heavily wounded we had left behind at Campton, under care of two physicians.[263] Early today we broke camp. Soon we came to Princeton, a fine small town with churches.[264] We had marched about ten miles and here made camp.

April 29th. We left early. All went well until we came to a swamp about 6 miles long. We had to go through because the other road were made dangerous by the rebs. We heard a few cannon shots but marched on toward the river Saline. The river was deep and Pontoon bridges had to be built. The entire night we had heavy rain and thunderstorms. Roads were terrible and we had to stop in the morass. Bum-Boom, suddenly the cannon barked behind us. Fear and trembling was upon the faces of the white people and more so upon those of the slaves who fled with us. We were in the morass and the enemy upon us. We muddled on until we were in the deepest mud and water and close to the swollen Saline River.[265] We made Bivouac on a small

263. One of those surgeons was William C. Finlaw, who was commissioned assistant surgeon of the Eighteenth Iowa Infantry on July 2, 1863, but declined the position. He accepted a similar position with the Second Missouri Light Artillery and served as the unit's assistant surgeon until discharged on February 2, 1865. Finlaw died on November 17, 1905, in Santa Rosa, California. William L. Nicholson, surgeon of the Twenty-ninth Iowa Infantry, reported that as the Federals prepared to abandon Camden, "about twenty-five or thirty of the worst cases were left in charge of Doctor Finlaw." *The history of Clinton County, Iowa, containing a history of the county, its cities, towns, &c., biographical sketches of citizens* (Chicago: Western Historical Company, 1879), 468; Adjutant General's Office, *Official army register of the volunteer force of the United States Army for the years 1861, '62, '63, '64, '65* (Washington DC: Government Printing Office, 1867), 7:64; *Journal of the American Medical Association* 45 (December 2, 1905), http://jama.ama-assn.org/cgi/reprint/XLV/1750.pdf; William L. Nicholson, "The Engagement at Jenkins' Ferry," *Annals of Iowa* 11 (October 1914): 505.

264. Dallas County was formed on January 1, 1845, and its seat was established at Dallaston, a name changed to Princeton in November 1845. The town was incorporated on March 4, 1849. Princeton did not survive the Civil War. Thelma Mays Coleman, "Princeton: Site of First County Seat, Town and Post Office," *Fordyce News Advocate*, November 19, 1986, p. 4C; Michael Hodge, "Dallas County," *Encyclopedia of Arkansas History & Culture*, http://www.encyclopediaofarkansas.net/encyclopedia/entry-detail.aspx?entryID=764.

265. Edward Ruegger wrote of the camp on April 29: "In the evening we again took bivouac, and what bivouac! We already stood up to our knees in water and mire, and still it rained on. To lie down was out of the question. Standing I leaned against a tree and soon fell asleep for a short time." Ruegger, "Five Weeks of My Army Life," 7.

farm. With darkness the cannonade ceased. We had to wait until under great difficulty the Pioneers made a bridge across the river. Then our large train, artillery and all that could walk and crawl crossed the river. Rain had been and was still pouring continually. We had slept a little lying on fence-rails. We had nothing to eat and had marched 21 miles.

April 30th (The Battle)

Early in the morning it was still raining. The water stood almost over the fence rails we slept on. We and many of the wagons had not crossed the river. No eats and little hope to soon cross the river. Firing behind us began again and soon appeared to be skirmish fire. If the rebels now came to attack, then our situation surely became serious if not hopeless. We had to remain in the swamp and await the things to come. Soon order came to be ready, to form battle line and then we went through mud and water across the little field, toward the small strip of bush and a little clearing beyond.

Here, at the edge of the woods we stopped, to let the troops of the First Brigade, who had done the skirmishing, go back. The 29th Iowa regiment had gone into the timber and was firing. By this time bullets whizzed around us. Our entire Brigade soon was in line and under increasing fire. The rebels came closer. Now they were in strong numbers on the small clearing and came closer every second. The rolling of the guns sounded like a continuous thunderstorm. Continual hissing and shrieking of thousands of bullets. The 29th Iowa began to waver and to retreat before the superior forces of the rebels. Then appeared our General Reiss and ordered us into the fray. With zest and hurrah, guns in hand we broke through the other regiment to meet the rebels in the open field. Terrible was the gunfire as we turned upon the surprised rebels. This they had not expected. They were sure of victory. Now they ran under terrible losses. Our bullets trimmed their lines and the rest fled in confusion. When they had been repulsed we were ordered back to the edge of the woods.[266]

We were the tip of the right wing and rested on a deep ditch full of water with bush on our left wing toward the river, bush hiding the ditch. The terrain did not permit us to bring cannon into action. Cannon would have sunk in the mud. It was much the same with the enemy. With great effort they, however, brought three cannon into play, against our right wing, in their second attack. But only about three times did their cannon speak, then their men and horses lay dead. Newly arrived negroes and other of our forces drove them back. They had come to about 60 steps from our position at the edge of the woods.[267]

Before the second attack the rebels had sent a division across the ditch, to our right, to cut off our retreat. Several times bullets

266. Edward Ruegger offered this version of this attack: "'Fall in,' was the command. We stood there about five minutes when the advance guard came running and lined up right and left to our regiment as well as they could; the rain of bullets already took its victims, and a 'Forward March'! command came. We knew what we had to expect. In front of us was a clearing, maybe comprising 100 acres, behind us the woods. When we reached the clearing, we furiously charged the enemy with bayonets and with such a resounding battle cry, which is only possible in such circumstances. We ran over the field and [dispersed] the enemy without firing one shot." Ruegger, "Five Weeks of My Army Life," 8. The initial attack was made by General Thomas Churchill's division. The nature of the terrain forced Churchill to deploy his brigades piecemeal, which helped the Union defenders break up that assault. Derek Allen Clements, "Engagement at Jenkins' Ferry," *Encyclopedia of Arkansas History &Culture*, http://www.encyclopediaofarkansas.net/encyclopedia/entry-detail.aspx?search=1&entryID=1136.

267. A section of Ruffner's Missouri Battery was brought into action and promptly charged by the Second Kansas Colored Infantry—its men screaming "Poison Springs!"—and the Twenty-ninth Iowa Infantry. The Kansas troops bayoneted three men who were trying to surrender and after the fight some wandered the battlefield, killing wounded Confederates. Urwin, "Poison Spring and Jenkins' Ferry," 130–32. Captain Ruegger wrote of the action: "Our regiment captured in these days a rebel battery and one regimental flag. The battery swung into action about 200 yards in front of our regiment; the Colonel ordered companies A and D to give the horses a volley and promptly we captured the same. The enemy's infantry was at hand, too, but too late. We held them in check until the rest of our negro regiment (two companies), after killing the artillerymen with their bayonets, had brought it behind our battle line. It was a sad spectacle, such a butchery, but they were right— they received no consideration and therefore did not give any." Ruegger, "Five Weeks of My Army Life," 10.

came from that direction but we could not see anybody and did not pay attention until it became annoying. Then without command our company A. turned and fired into the dark timber from where the bullets came. Some said they were our troops but we did not believe it. Soon we heard command, saw the rebels and now strong firing ensued from both sides. The rebs made ready to come across the ditch, when suddenly the negroes came to our aid. Part of the negroes crossed the ditch and met the rebels. These now fled pursued by the colored soldiers.[268]

Now the second frontal attack began with the cannon aiding.[269] The rebels had been driven back at our wing. It was now quiet here and companies A. and B. were now sent to advance and to locate the enemy.[270] We came almost across the field and to the edge of the woods without firing and then took position behind trees and stumps. Now loud and strong cannonade came from the left wing. Warning came to watch keenly for it would come against us. Soon we saw the woods full of advancing rebels who seeing us so close, at once opened fire. We dodged where we could and ran through the timber back to our battle line. Bullets whizzed around us and mud splashed over us. Our men feared we would all be killed but as far as I know only one was seriously wounded. We went for a new supply of ammunition[271] and then back

268. Colonel Samuel J. Crawford of the Second Kansas Colored Infantry wrote of this movement: "Perceiving the enemy were endeavoring to flank our lines on the right, I detached Capt. Frank Kister with two companies (D and C), directing him to cross a deep slough or ravine on my right, engage the enemy, and check his movements in that direction at all hazards. The order was promptly obeyed by the captain executing the movement under a very heavy fire from the enemy and under circumstances which would try the nerves of old soldiers, effecting the object desired." *OR*, 34, part 1:758.

269. The second Confederate attack was made by Major General Mosby M. Parsons' Missouri division. Clements, "Engagement at Jenkins' Ferry."

270. Captain Ruegger noted: "After each attack, each regiment sent two companies forward as [illegible] and as such we sneaked towards the rebels' battle line, sometimes as close as fifty yards." Ruegger, "Five Weeks of My Army Life," 9.

271. General Salomon reported: "The enemy, driven at every point, now opportunely gave us a few moments' time in which to replenish our supply of ammunition. This was brought up from the rear by mounted troopers, my own escort assisting." *OR*, 34, part 1:690.

to battle line, where just now the rebels were being repulsed for the third time. We were now sideways and saw some rebels who did not want to retreat and shot from behind trees. We fired, and quickly, under our loud laughter, they fled. The third attack of the rebels had been made on the entire line, with the whole force, but again they met severe repulse.[272]

End of the Battle.

After this the rebels withdrew nine miles because they believed we had received re-enforcements and might pursue them. We were glad that the fight was over and that we now could go back and try to satisfy our great hunger. We returned through mud knee deep. Our wagons were sunken in mud and on fire. We went right to the bridge, rested and waited to let all cross over that could be moved. Then the bridge was destroyed to head off pursuit.[273] We had now no wagons to take along the bridge nor mules to pull such load. When all was accomplished and the bridge destroyed we took up our march but nothing but mud and water. Our mules because of long hunger sunk into the mud and had to be abandoned. Sometimes even others drove over them. Some mules were still kicking in the mud. All was left the way it lay. The road was full of wagons, animals, boxes; full of good things, wagons full of old and new uniforms, barrels of coffee and many other things. All was left in the mud sunken, burning and much of it ashes. The road was full of precious things large and small, dead

272. The final attack of the day was made by Walker's Texas Division. Clements, "Engagement at Jenkins' Ferry."

273. Captain Junius B. Wheeler, chief engineer of Steele's army, wrote of the decision to destroy the pontoon bridges: "The mules could scarcely pull the wagons, much less when loaded, and over such a road it was impossible to get it along. The pontoons were very much the worse for wear, and several were worn out, so as no longer to be reliable. It was destroyed by cutting each compartment with an ax and piercing them with the bayonet. Many of the chesses were split with axes and then thrown in the stream, and some of the balks were thrown in after cutting them in two parts. The bridge was dismantled by successive rafts and destroyed by detail." OR, 34, part 1:677–78.

and living and half dead under inhuman suffering. Men and animals were dying.—[274]

As last we came out of the swamp onto higher ground and camp was made at once. It was night. Our Brigade had lost about 500 men in dead, wounded and missed. The loss of our regiment was 128.[275] Our company A. lost two dead and six wounded.[276] Two of the latter fell into the hands of the rebels because they remained with the severely wounded, and when we were gone the rebels took them.[277] The battle lasted six hours, from six A.M. until noon.

The loss of the rebels, according to their own statements, was about 2000 in dead and wounded, among them one Major General and two other Generals.[278] We took 3 cannon, 4 flags from the

274. Michael Zimmer wrote: "Most horses and mules gave up. It was terrible to see how the exhausted and starving animals got stuck in the mud and collapsed in the middle of the road. Thus you could see hardly more than just their heads sticking out of the mud now and then. We had to [put] them out of their misery." Macha and Wolf, *Michael Zimmer's Diary*, 196. Andrew Sperry of the Thirty-Third Iowa observed: "Many as were the wagons that had been destroyed, the train still stretched out apparently two or three miles.... When a wagon stuck—and all the wagons were constantly sticking—every endeavor was made to raise it out of the mud and get it moving again. If all means failed, the mules were unhitched and the wagon broken and burned; and so all over the swamp, near the road, were burning wagons and their scattered contents." Urwin and Urwin, *History of the 33d Iowa*, 110.

275. The First Brigade of the Third Division, which included the Ninth Wisconsin, suffered 44 killed, 331 wounded, and 18 missing at Jenkins' Ferry. The Ninth Wisconsin had 14 killed and 71 wounded. *OR*, 34, part 1:692.

276. From Company A, Ninth Wisconsin Infantry, Corporal Christian Kaiser and Private John Schilling were killed and Privates Henry Meyer, John Mueller, David Duerrow, Michael Tiesach, Robert Frederick [Friedrich], and Fred Wendlorff [Ferdinand Wendorff] were wounded at Jenkins' Ferry. Quiner, *Military History of Wisconsin*, 546.

277. Robert Friedrich and Ferdinand Wendorff were the two Company A men made prisoner at Jenkins' Ferry. *Roster of Wisconsin Volunteers*, 606, 608.

278. Incomplete Confederate reports show losses of 86 killed, 356 wounded, and one missing; the actual total was almost certainly considerably higher. Clements, "Engagement at Jenkins' Ferry." Among the Confederate dead were Brigadier General William R. Scurry and Colonel Horace Randal, both of whom led Texas brigades and were mortally wounded. Brigadier General Thomas W. Waul, another Texas brigade commander, was wounded at Jenkins' Ferry. Bearss, *Steele's Retreat from Camden*, 166.

rebels.[279] Brigade General Solomon was our commander during the battle as well as before. Brigade General Rice was severely wounded in the second attack and our Major E. Solomon had to take the command of our Brigade.[280] The strength of the rebels was about 24,000 under General Kirby Schmidt and other Generals.[281] Our strength was about 5000 men.[282] Our cavalry was near Little Rock to attack the rebel cavalry, who were threatening the city.[283]

May 1. Today, after a good night's rest, we have a better day, not in provision but in weather and we are willing to move on. The ground is soft and full of water but better than yesterday. We march easier, for all our baggage is thrown away and lost. Neither have we any provisions to carry inside nor in our knapsacks. But we have hope. Now it is getting night and we are still marching on. At ten o'clock, when it was very dark, call came "Lie down." Quietly we made fire. Most of us have only what we have on. Some even have no shoes. We have nothing to eat. We have marched 25 miles and 30 more to go.

279. Wagoner John Welhaupt and Private William Ohler of Company B, Ninth Wisconsin, captured one of the Confederate flags at Jenkins' Ferry. *Military History of Wisconsin*, 546. Two others were captured by the Fiftieth Indiana Infantry, also in Rice's brigade. *OR*, 34, part 1:698. The flags were almost certainly those of Arkansas regiments under Brigadier General Thomas Churchill who were pinned down by the Ninth Wisconsin at Jenkins' Ferry, and the Wisconsin Veterans Museum returned the flag captured by the Ninth Wisconsin to Arkansas in 2001. The conserved flag is now on display in the Arkansas National Guard Museum at Camp Robinson in North Little Rock. Steve Rucker, email to author, July 23, 2012.

280. Rice was shot in the foot during the second Confederate assault, as he moved toward the left of his lines. Colonel Charles E. Salomon of the Ninth Wisconsin commanded the brigade for the remainder of the battle. *OR*, 34, part 1:698.

281. Kirby Smith had about 7,500 men involved in the fighting from the three divisions he commanded. Forsyth, *The Camden Expedition*, 162–68.

282. Steele reported that "the number of our troops engaged [at Jenkins' Ferry] did not exceed 4,000." *OR*, 34, part 1:607.

283. Brigadier General Eugene A. Carr, fearing that Brigadier General James F. Fagan's Confederate horsemen would attack Little Rock while the main army was engaged on the Saline River, hurried toward Little Rock, arriving at the capital at 5 a.m. on May 1, 1864. While the anticipated cavalry battle did not extend beyond a skirmish at Whitmore's Mill, Carr's arrival in Little Rock did result in rations being sent toward the starving Union army as it struggled north from Jenkins' Ferry. Bearrs, *Steele's Retreat from Camden*, 170–71.

May 2nd. Early we started over hill and valley through fields and woods. We pass farms and have good roads and courageously go on. Soldiers who do not fear the enemy do not lose courage when they have to fast a few days. Despite hunger we crack jokes. At last we are on the Telegraph Road to Little Rock and Benton. With new courage we press on. Soon we make camp on a large field, where we had our first camp, at the beginning of the expedition. Here we are to remain during the coming night. Many can go no farther because too tired and worn.

Crackers and Little Rock

It was nearly night when suddenly a rush came into camp. All the lame and discouraged ran in one direction as if they were new men. Hurrah! Crackers! Plenty crackers. Now we get hurrah! It came from all directions. Several loads of crackers had arrived from Little Rock. In greatest hurry they were unloaded and distributed. Joy every where and then sweet sleep.[284]

May 3rd. This morning all formed orderly. Our company ahead. Then came a company of negroes with the captured cannon and flags. Then came the first Brigade and so the entire army. Soon we came to a little hill from which we can overlook the city. Here we waited until all had arrived and then, between thousands of happy faces, with music, we marched into the city and entered our well known camp of tent houses. Now we could eat and drink and then rested from the great 276 mile expedition.[285]

284. Michael Zimmer wrote on May 2: "Some horses were sent to Little Rock to get some crackers for us so that we would have something to eat in the evening. Late in the night they returned and brought what we wanted. Immediately orderly call was sounded and every company got a box of crackers. The rejoicing and the shouting of hoorays seemed like they would not end, when the crackers appeared, and we were so happy with them." Macha and Wolf, *Michael Zimmer's Diary*, 197.

285. Zimmer wrote: "Today at 6 o'clock we left for Little Rock and arrived there at noon. The platoon was arranged and we went marching at parade step through the town. First the two captured cannons and two Secessionist flags came, then our regiment, then the other regiments in the order they were arranged in brigades. Thus one brigade followed the other, and we marched to our camp. Oh, how happy I was when I could move into my cosy tent." Macha and Wolf, *Michael Zimmer's Diary*, 197. Captain Ruegger remembered: "The next day in the afternoon we arrived in Little Rock, each fort firing…honor salvos. All the troops were lined up at attention, and we marched through the whole city between presented arms. But, how did we look! Some did not have any hats, others no shoes, others no coats, others torn pants—in short, we looked like a corps of bandits; but one thing all of us still possessed—our weapons." Ruegger, "Five Weeks of My Army Life," 10.

The Work & Trip to Pine Bluff.

May 24. After our arrival at [Little Rock] we had two weeks of rest. Then service was taken up again. We had to build defenses around town. Much digging and shoveling was done to make the city safe against attack, for surprise attack was feared. Forts and ditches were made all around the city. Batteries are placed. It is much work. The timber for miles around has to be cut to head off unseen approach of an enemy.

Besides we have to load and unload the boats and work in commission stores.

May 25th. Today we were ordered as guards on a boat under Major General Steel on a trip down the Arkansas River, to Pine Bluff. The vista along the river changes from beautiful plantations to the wild and romantic. Often 5 to 30 negro huts [stone huts] in one row, and a flock of woolly headed children, out of black eyes peering at us. We see many wild geese and ducks but even more Turkey Buzzards. They devour the many dead carcasses lying around.

Toward evening we reached Pine Bluff. Cannon greeted us and many people were along the shore to look at our General Staff. We were received by the commander of the place, Col. Clayton, who had often proven himself a hero, at this place.[286] We remained on the boat. Next day great review was held over all the forces. We were on-lookers. Pine Bluff is a fine and well-fortified town, and has withstood many attacks

286. Powell Clayton was born in Bethel Township, Pennsylvania, on August 7, 1833, and moved to Leavenworth, Kansas, in 1855 for work as a surveyor. Joining the Union army in May 1861, Clayton led a company of Kansas infantry at Wilson's Creek in 1861 and was commissioned lieutenant colonel of the Fifth Kansas Cavalry in February 1862. Clayton's Fifth Kansas fought guerrillas around Helena in 1862 and 1863 before occupying Pine Bluff in September 1863. He was promoted to brigadier general on August 1, 1864. Clayton was Arkansas's Reconstruction governor and active in Republican politics for the rest of his life. He died in Washington DC on August 25, 1914, and is buried in Arlington National Cemetery. Carl H. Moneyhon, "Powell Clayton," *Encyclopedia of Arkansas History & Culture*, http://www.encyclopediaofarkansas.net/encyclopedia/entry-detail.aspx?search=1&entryID=94.

of the rebels. It shows many bullet marks.[287] Here we found many negro women and children.[288]

On the 29th we returned to Little Rock and arrived at 11:00 p.m. — It is now July and we are still fortifying the city and doing work on the Levee. We are doing picket work, watch in town and river front keeps us busy. It is very hot and we have again built tents from brush. Board summer houses are being built. We dug a well and found better water. All is well and in fine shape.

The Sickness.

August. Sickness is beginning to encroach into our regiment and even into the entire army. It is called scorbut [scurvy]. The symptoms are red, blue, and even green blotches on the body mostly on the lower limbs and the gums. On some the legs are swollen and blue, green and black. The gums are turning black and sponge-like. Under least pressure blood oozes out and the gums fall off as if rotten. Many unfit for service and must be sent home.[289]

Furlough and Trip Home. After I was in the grip of the disease and unfit for service for several weeks, I, with many others, was offered a furlough and took it. It could not be cured unless under different diet. This could not be had in the army. Thirty men of our regiment had left before

287. Pine Bluff had suffered extensively in the October 25, 1863, battle in which much of the town had been burned. Clayton wrote after the fighting that "there is scarcely a house in town that does not show the effects of battle," while a Wisconsin officer observed that "the town shows the marks of a hard fight, many of the houses being riddled with shot." Christ, *Civil War Arkansas, 1863*, 242–43.

288. As with most other Union bases in Arkansas, Pine Bluff was a magnet for slaves who fled area plantations to seek freedom and the protection of the army. The Federals established camps for them east and west of town. Christ, *Civil War Arkansas, 1863*, 227–28.

289. Scurvy, a disease caused largely by a lack of fresh vegetables in the diet, was widespread in the Union army in Arkansas in 1864. The base at DeValls Bluff reported 2,277 cases of scurvy between January 1 and September 1, 1864, of which 14 were fatal. Paul E. Steiner, *Disease in the Civil War: Natural Biological Warfare in 1861–1865* (Springfield, IL: Charles C. Thomas, 1968), 226.

this and seven more were waiting for their passes, and I was one of them.[290] At last our permits arrived and on August 13th we left Little Rock on the train. At 1:00 o'clock we arrived at Duvall's Bluff. This town has grown rapidly. When we saw it earlier it was nothing.[291] Here we took the steamer "Kate Hart"[292] and had to lie there all day. At 3:00 P.M. August 14th we left. The night was bright and we went on. At 3:00 A.M. we arrived at Clarksville.[293] Here we had to wait till morning. Here two cannon.

On the 15th in the evening we came out of the White River into the Mississippi and there rested for ½ hour, at the cannon boats, and registered according to law.

On the 16th at 1:00 p.m. we came to Helena, stopped two hours and then went on. On the 17th we came within 10 miles of Memphis, Tenn. Here our engine broke down and we could not proceed. Another boat towed us and brought us to Memphis. From here we boarded a fine large steamer, the "City of Alton."[294] A while after we were on

290. Haas's muster roll for July and August 1864 show him absent with leave. The September and October roll declares him "absent on sick furlough at Wis." Compiled Service Records, supplied by Michael Wilson.

291. As the eastern terminus of the only operating railroad in Arkansas and an important White River port, DeValls Bluff became a major Union base after August 1863. In addition to the many buildings erected to serve the soldiers based there, DeValls Bluff also contained a large refugee population. Goodspeed states that "by the close of the war the place contained many buildings and had a large population, mostly of refugees." *Biographical and Historical Memoirs of Eastern Arkansas* (Chicago: Goodspeed Publishing Co., 1890), 680.

292. The 279-ton sternwheel paddleboat *Kate Hart* was early in its service on the White River, having been built in 1864 in Paducah, Kentucky. After the war, its hull as used as a sand barge in Pittsburgh, Pennsylvania, and later, after a boiler and machinery were added, as a mechanized sand-and-gravel dredge. Way, *Way's Packet Directory*, 266.

293. Since Clarksville lies a considerable distance west on the Arkansas River, Haas is surely referring to Clarendon on the White River here.

294. The *City of Alton*, a sternwheel paddleboat built at Madison, Indiana, in 1860, had a proud war record. In April 1861, when secessionists threatened the St. Louis Armory, it was used to transport more than 20,000 muskets, 5,000 carbines, 500 revolvers, 100,000 cartridges, and other equipment across the Mississippi to Alton, Illinois, a feat accomplished when U.S. Army commanders put out a rumor that the materiel was being moved from the armory via streetcar. It later served with U. S. Grant's army in Tennessee and ran from St. Louis to Memphis after the war. Way, *Way's Packet Directory*, 89; Christopher Phillips, *Damned Yankee: The Life of General Nathaniel Lyon* (Columbia: University of Missouri Press, 1990), 166–67.

board rumor came that two women were among the soldiers, dressed as men. Everybody went on deck to see them. I too was keenly interested and went. There in the midst of a group of soldiers sat a very young and beautiful soldier, who in manner, voice and carriage had nothing of the man soldier and now was discovered as not belonging here. Upon inquiry she stated that she had served 18 months as soldier, first as tambour[295] and then as teamster. She received rich presents from soldiers and civil travelers. Her hair shorn short, and in soldier's uniform and assuming rough manners, she had not been detected.

Now let us look at the other one at the rear of the ship. She was telling fortune from cards. She was rather old for a soldier and had too much bust for a man and could not hide it. The fine lines of the face too were a telltale nor could she hide it in her voice. She had served two years in a cavalry regiment and had been wounded in one hand. Next came time for battle. She refused to go in and revealed her Identity. She was dismissed from service, was brought to the boat under escort to be sent home to Missouri. The escort gave away the secret. The first one was very much minded to re-enlist.

At 5:00 o'clock in the evening we left Memphis and made fine progress up the river, all night, and at 4:00 o'clock next morning came to Columbus, Ky. At 9:00 P.M. to Cairo, where we landed. On the 19th, at 2:00 A.M. we boarded the train of the Central Railroad and at 11:00 o'clock at night we reached Chicago, where we spent the night in a hotel.

Out trip, 365 miles, was through all varieties of country and civilization. On the 20th at 10:00 o'clock we left Chicago and came to Milwauke (a distance of 85 miles) at 1:00 o'clock P.M. On the 22nd, at 8:00 in the evening, I boarded the boat "The Sea Bird"[296] and at 11:00 o'clock came to Post Washington. From here, on the 24th I left for home.

295. *Tambour* is German for drummer.
296. Haas may be mistaken about the identity of this vessel. The only *Sea Bird* listed in *Way's Packet Directory* was burned and sunk at Cape Girardeau, Missouri, in 1848. Way, *Way's Packet Directory*, 421.

After several trips to Sheboygan and Mactisaw [?] I came at last, with several others of our regiment, to Milwauke, where we, in November awaited the arrival of our regiment to be discharged. The time of our enlistment had ended in October.

Return of the Regiment.

On Nov. 17th 1864 came the long looked for order that all who did not care to re-enlist shall make ready.[297] (This had been done some time ago. The order came afterward.) Then all marched into town, where General Stell addressed the regiment.[298] Then we marched to the prison to take a large number of rebel prisoners to St. Louis. Our men were on top of the cars and the prisoners in them. We traveled in pouring rain and at last came to Duvall's Bluff, and remained over night. Next morning we departed and did not stop until on the 21st we came to Memphis, where we remained till next day. On the 23 we came to Columbus and late that day to Cairo, Illinois. From here, 70 of the weakest were put on the Central Railroad and arrived at Milwauke on the 25th, and remained there.

The others with the prisoners left Cairo on the 24th, going up the Mississippi and came to St. Louis on the 26th. From there they pro-

---

297. According to Michael Zimmer, discipline had declined in the Ninth Wisconsin as they awaited their orders to return home. He wrote on November 1: "The boys knew exactly that their time to serve was over and that they had long enough been tyrannized by the aristocratic gentlemen officers. That was why they did not want to drill any longer, which even the officers had to accept." Macha and Wolf, *Michael Zimmer's Diary*, 206.

298. According to Zimmer, Friedrich Salomon first addressed the regiment, saying, "I thank you, comrades, with all my heart for your perseverance and your courage, which you have shown every time it was necessary. I am proud to have been the creator of the 9th Wisconsin Regiment." They then marched to Frederick Steele's headquarters, where the general "appeared on a balcony where he gave a short speech. He regretted to bid farewell to such brave men, but he hoped we would return to his command soon, whereupon we presented arms and gave him three hoorays." Macha and Wolf, *Michael Zimmer's Diary*, 207.

ceeded to Alton, Illinois, where they delivered the prisoners.[299] They left there on the 27th and came to Chicago on the 28th. The same day, they left for Milwauke and were received there at 2:00 p.m.

At Milwauke a great reception was prepared. The cannon roared, banners waved and great crowds greeted the regiment as they marched through the city. On West Water Street a great banquet was prepared for the whole regiment. Great speeches were held honoring the brave soldiers. When all was over, each went his own way.[300]

The Discharge.

On December second 1864 we received our Discharge. Now we waited for our pay. On Dec. 5th we were paid in full and $100.00 bounty. We had served three years and three months. Now each one could stop as long as he pleased and go where and when he wanted.

On my return on Nov. 2nd, I reached home—30 miles from Madison, stopping at Millers.

Later returning to meet the regiment after discharge, I arrived at home on December 11th 1864.

299. An Illinois state prison had been established at Alton in 1831, but it was abandoned because it was located in an unhealthy location. The site was reopened early in the Civil War to serve as a prisoner-of-war camp, where it became infamous for overcrowding and widespread disease. About 20 percent of the Confederate soldiers imprisoned there died. Alton prison was demolished after the Civil War. Garrison, *The Encyclopedia of Civil War Usage*, 9. Michael Zimmer reported that the regiment escorted 220 Confederate prisoners there. He wrote that when they "reached St. Louis [they] thought we could get rid of our prisoners, but we were wrong, as there was no place for them. We had to take them with us to Alton, Illinois, where they were put into the city jail. We were happy to leave them there." Macha and Wolf, *Michael Zimmer's Diary*, 207–8.

300. Michael Zimmer wrote of the celebration: "[We] reached Milwaukee at 2 o'-clock in the afternoon. When we reached the station, we were welcomed by several gunshots. We got out immediately and the regiment fell in....We marched on at once, of course with a band ahead. We stopped at the Republican house and we were ordered: Stack arms! We were taken by a committee to a great hall where we found a long table for each company with everything one could wish. There was no lack of Phillip Baest's lager either. In the evening we had a free ball, where everyone had great fun." Macha and Wolf, *Michael Zimmer's Diary*, 208–9.

Photographs and Maps

Frederick Saloman, whose brother was the governor of Wisconsin, led the Ninth Wisconsin Infantry Regiment until his promotion to brigadier general in 1862. (Courtesy of the Butler Center for Arkansas Studies, Central Arkansas Library System, Little Rock)

Jacob Haas. (Courtesy of Michael Wilson)

Jacob Haas and his second wife, Augusta.
(Courtesy of Michael Wilson)

General James Gilpatrick Blunt led the Army of the Frontier, which included the Ninth Wisconsin Infantry Regiment, in actions in Arkansas, Missouri, and the Indian Territory. (Courtesy of Wilson's Creek National Battlefield)

Charles Saloman took his brother Frederick's place at the head of the Ninth Wisconsin Infantry Regiment after Frederick's promotion, and he would lead the regiment through most of its battles. (Courtesy of Kent Saloman)

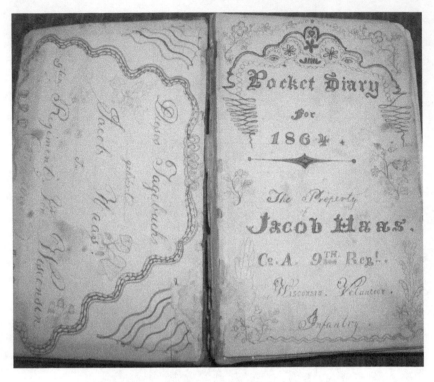

Jacob Haas's pocket diary for 1864. (Courtesy of Michael Wilson)

Another hand-illustrated page of Jacob Haas's 1864 diary.
(Courtesy of Michael Wilson)

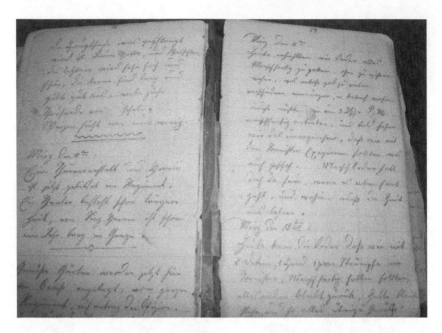

Jacob Haas's son-in-law translated the diary from the original German between 1920 and 1940. (Courtesy of Michael Wilson)

Major General Frederick Steele led a Union army from Little Rock to southwest Arkansas in the spring of 1864, a failed expedition that culminated in the battle of Jenkins' Ferry. (Courtesy of the Butler Center for Arkansas Studies, Central Arkansas Library System, Little Rock, Arkansas)

*Jacob Haas and the Ninth Wisconsin Infantry Regiment
marched hundreds of miles through rugged territory
in Kansas, Missouri, northwest Arkansas, and the
Indian Territory in 1862 and 1863. Stars indicate where
battles occurred.* (Map courtesy of Tony Feaster)

This map shows the travels of Jacob Haas and the Ninth Wisconsin Infantry Regiment in Arkansas in 1863 and 1864. (Map courtesy of Tony Feaster)

Bibliography

Adjutant General's Office. *Official Army Register of the Volunteer Force of the United States Army for the Years 1861, '62, '63, '64, '65*. Washington DC: Government Printing Office, 1867.

Adjutant General's Office. *Roster of Wisconsin Volunteers, War of the Rebellion, 1861–1865*. Madison, WI: Democrat Printing Co., 1886.

Arey, Frank. "Action at Moscow." *Encyclopedia of Arkansas History & Culture*. http://www.encyclopediaofarkansas.net/encyclopedia/entry-detail.aspx?search=1&entryID=2513 (accessed October 3, 2013).

Arkansas Natural Heritage Commission. "Extinct Animals (Historic Period)." *Encyclopedia of Arkansas History & Culture*. http://www.encyclopediaofarkansas.net/encyclopedia/entry-detail.aspx?search=1&entryID=2624 (accessed October 3, 2013).

Arkansas (Map). New York: J. H. Colton and Co., 1855.

Banasik, Michael E. *Reluctant Cannoneer: The Diary of Robert T. McMahan of the Twenty-fifth Independent Ohio Light Artillery*. Iowa City, IA: Press of the Camp Pope Bookshop, 2000.

Bearden, Russell E. "Pine Bluff (Jefferson County)." *Encyclopedia of Arkansas History & Culture*. http://www.encyclopediaofarkansas.net/encyclopedia/entry-detail.aspx?search=1&entryID=908 (accessed December 13, 2013).

Bearss, Edwin C. "The Battle of Helena, July 4, 1863." *Arkansas Historical Quarterly* 20 (Autumn 1961).

————. *Steele's Retreat from Camden and the Battle of Jenkins' Ferry*. Little Rock: Pioneer Press, 1967.

Bell, James W. "Little Rock (Pulaski County)." *Encyclopedia of Arkansas History & Culture*. http://www.encyclopediaofarkansas.net/encyclopedia/entry-detail.aspx?entryID=970 (accessed October 3, 2013).

Biographical and Historical Memoirs of Eastern Arkansas. Chicago: The Goodspeed Publishing Co., 1890.

Bishop, A. W. *Loyalty on the Frontier or Sketches of Union Men of the South-West with Incidents and Adventures in Rebellion on the Border*, edited by Kim Allen Scott. Fayetteville: University of Arkansas Press, 2003.

Blackmar, Frank Wilson. *Kansas; a cyclopedia of state history, embracing events, institutions, industries, counties, cities, towns, prominent persons, etc. ... with a supplementary volume devoted to selected personal history and reminiscence.* Chicago: Standard Publishing Co., 1912.

Britton, Wiley. *The Union Indian Brigade in the Civil War.* Kansas City, MO: Franklin Hudson, 1922.

Castel, Albert. *Civil War Kansas: Reaping the Whirlwind.* Lawrence: University Press of Kansas, 1997.

Christ, Mark K. "Action at Bentonville." *Encyclopedia of Arkansas History & Culture.* http://www.encyclopediaofarkansas.net/encyclopedia/entry-detail.aspx?search=1&entryID=510 (accessed December 13, 2013).

———. *Civil War Arkansas, 1863: The Battle for a State.* Norman: University of Oklahoma Press, 2010.

———. "The Federals Fought Like Devils." *North and South* 12, no. 6 (March 2011).

———. *"The Homer* (Shipwreck)." National Register of Historic Places nomination, Arkansas Historic Preservation Program, Little Rock, 2002.

———. "Skirmishes at Okolona." *Encyclopedia of Arkansas History & Culture.* http://www.encyclopediaofarkansas.net/encyclopedia/entry-detail.aspx?search=1&entryID=4442 (accessed December 13, 2013).

———. "'Them dam'd gunboats': A Union Sailor's Letters from the Arkansas Post Expedition." *Arkansas Historical Quarterly* 66 (Winter 2007).

Christ, Mark K., ed. *"All Cut to Pieces and Gone to Hell": The Civil War, Race Relations, and the Battle of Poison Spring.* Little Rock: August House/Butler Center, 2003.

———. *The Earth Reeled and Trees Trembled: Civil War Arkansas 1863–1864.* Little Rock: Old State House Museum, 2007.

———. *Rugged and Sublime: The Civil War in Arkansas.* Fayetteville: University of Arkansas Press, 1994.

Cleek, Katherine. "Van Winkle Mill Site." National Register of Historic Places nomination, Arkansas Historic Preservation Program, Little Rock, 2007.

Clements, Derek Allen. "Engagement at Jenkins' Ferry." *Encyclopedia of Arkansas History & Culture.* http://www.encyclopediaofarkansas.net/encyclopedia/entry-detail.aspx?search=1&entryID=1136 (accessed December 13, 2013).

Coleman, Thelma Mays. "Princeton: Site of First County Seat, Town and Post Office." *Fordyce News Advocate*, November 19, 1986.

Conard, Howard L., ed. *Encyclopedia of the History of Missouri*, vol. 1. New York: Southern History Company, 1901.

Confer, Clarissa W. *The Cherokee Nation in the Civil War*. Norman: University of Oklahoma Press, 2007.

Coombe, Jack D. *Thunder Along the Mississippi: The River Battles That Split the Confederacy*. New York: Sarpedon, 1996.

DeBlack, Thomas A. *With Fire and Sword: Arkansas, 1861–1874*. Fayetteville: University of Arkansas Press, 2003.

Duncan, L. Wallace, and Charles F. Scott, ed. and comp. *History of Allen and Woodson Counties Kansas*. Iola, KS: Iola Register, 1901.

Dyer, Frederick H. *A Compendium of the War of the Rebellion*. 3 parts. Des Moines, IA: F. H. Dyer, 1908; facsimile reprint, Dayton, OH: Broadfoot Publishing Co., 1994.

Earngey, Bill. *Missouri Roadsides: The Traveler's Companion*. Columbia: University of Missouri Press, 1995.

Edwards, Whit. *"The Prairie was on Fire": Eyewitness Accounts of the Civil War in the Indian Territory*. Oklahoma City: Oklahoma Historical Society, 2001.

Engle, Stephen D. *Yankee Dutchman: The Life of Franz Sigel*. Fayetteville: University of Arkansas Press, 1993.

Evans, Clement A., ed. *Confederate Military History Extended Edition, Vol. XII Missouri*. Confederate Publishing Co., 1899; reprint with new material, Wilmington, NC: Broadfoot Publishing Co., 1988.

Ewing, Andrew. *An Oration Delivered on the Occasion of the Inauguration of the Bust erected to the Memory of Gen. Andrew Jackson in the City of Memphis, January 8, 1859*. Nashville: E. G. Eastman and Co., 1859.

Forsyth, Michael J. *The Camden Expedition of 1864 and the Opportunity Lost by the Confederacy to Change the Civil War*. Jefferson, NC: McFarland and Co., 2003.

Garrison, Webb, with Cheryl Garrison. *The Encyclopedia of Civil War Usage: An Illustrated Compendium of the Everyday Language of Soldiers and Civilians*. Nashville: Cumberland House, 2001.

Gaughan, J. E. "Historic Camden." *Arkansas Historical Quarterly* 20, no. 3 (Autumn 1961).

Granade, S. Ray. "Arkadelphia (Clark County). *Encyclopedia of Arkansas History & Culture.* http://www.encyclopediaofarkansas.net/encyclopedia/entry-detail.aspx?search=1&entryID=848 (accessed December 13, 2013).

Heidler, David S., and Jeanne T. Heidler, eds. *Encyclopedia of the American Civil War.* New York: W. W. Norton and Co., 2000.

The history of Clinton County, Iowa, containing a history of the county, its cities, towns, &c., biographical sketches of citizens. Chicago: Western Historical Company, 1879.

Hodge, Michael. "Dallas County." *Encyclopedia of Arkansas History & Culture.* http://www.encyclopediaofarkansas.net/encyclopedia/entry-detail.aspx?entryID=764 (accessed December 13, 2013).

Hope, Holly. "Rose Hill Cemetery." National Register of Historic Places nomination, Arkansas Historic Preservation Program, Little Rock, 1998.

Hughes, Michael A. "Wartime Gristmill Destruction in Northwest Arkansas and Military-Farm Colonies." *Arkansas Historical Quarterly* 46 (Summer 1987).

Hunt, Roger D., and Jack R. Brown. *Brevet Brigadiers in Blue.* Gaithersburg, MD: Olde Soldier Books, 1990.

Johnson's Kansas and Missouri (map). New York: Johnson and Ward, 1864.

Joiner, Gary D. *Mr. Lincoln's Brown Water Navy: The Mississippi Squadron.* Lanham, MD: Rowman and Littlefield, 2007.

Journal of the American Medical Association 45 (December 2, 1905).

Laster, Patricia Paulus. "Benton (Saline County)." *Encyclopedia of Arkansas History & Culture.* http://www.encyclopediaofarkansas.net/encyclopedia/entry-detail.aspx?entryID=979 (accessed December 13, 2013).

Long, E. B., with Barbara Long. *The Civil War Day By Day: An Almanac 1861–1865.* New York: Da Capo Press, 1971.

Lothrop, Charles. *A History of the First Iowa Cavalry Veteran Volunteers, From Its Organization in 1861 to Its Muster Out of the United States Service in 1866.* Lyons, IA: Beers & Eaton, 1890.

Love, William DeLoss. *Wisconsin in the War of the Rebellion; A History of All Regiments and Batteries.* Chicago: Church and Goodman, 1866.

Macha, Jurgen, and Andrea Wolf, ed. *Michael Zimmer's Diary: Ein Deutsches Tagebuch aus dem Amerikanischen Burgerkrieg.* Frankfurt: Peter Lang, 2001.

Mayo, W. R. "Clarendon (Monroe County)." *Encyclopedia of Arkansas History & Culture*. http://www.encyclopediaofarkansas.net/encyclopedia/entry-detail.aspx?search=1&entryID=942 (accessed December 13, 2013).

Missouri: The WPA Guide to the "Show Me" State. St. Louis: Missouri Historical Society Press, 1998.

Moneyhon, Carl H. "Powell Clayton (1833–1914)." *Encyclopedia of Arkansas History & Culture*. http://www.encyclopediaofarkansas.net/encyclopedia/entry-detail.aspx?search=1&entryID=94 (accessed December 13, 2013).

National Daily Democrat (Little Rock), March 26, 1864.

Nicholson, William L. "The Engagement at Jenkins' Ferry." *Annals of Iowa* 11 (October 1914).

Palmer, Patricia J. *Frederick Steele: Forgotten General*. Stanford, CA: Board of Trustees of Leland Stanford Junior University, 1971.

Phillips, Christopher. *Damned Yankee: The Life of General Nathaniel Lyon*. Columbia: University of Missouri Press, 1990.

Polston, Mike. "Carrollton (Carroll County)." *Encyclopedia of Arkansas History & Culture*. http://www.encyclopediaofarkansas.net/encyclopedia/entry-detail.aspx?search=1&entryID=6192 (accessed December 13, 2013).

———. "Brownsville (Lonoke County)." *Encyclopedia of Arkansas History & Culture*. http://www.encyclopediaofarkansas.net/encyclopedia/entry-detail.aspx?search=1&entryID=6088 (accessed December 13, 2013).

Popchock, Barry, ed. *Soldier Boy: The Civil War Letters of Charles O. Musser, 29th Iowa*. Iowa City: University of Iowa Press, 1995.

Potter, James E., and Edith Robbins, eds. *Marching with the First Nebraska: A Civil War Diary*. Norman: University of Oklahoma Press, 2007.

Quiner, E. B. *The Military History of Wisconsin: A Record of the Civil and Military Patriotism of the State, in the War for the Union*. Chicago: Clark and Company, 1866.

Quiner Scrapbooks: Correspondence of the Wisconsin Volunteers, 1861–1865, 2:30. Wisconsin State Historical Society.

Report of the Adjutant General of the State of Indiana, Vol. III: 1862–1865. Indianapolis: Samuel M. Douglas, State Printer, 1866.

Report of the Adjutant General of the State of Kansas, 1861–65. Topeka: Kansas State Printing Company, 1896.

"Rhea's Mill." *Flashback* 7, no. 4 (December 1962).

Ruegger, Edward. "Five Weeks of My Army Life." Wisconsin Historical Society Library and Archives, Madison, Wisconsin.

"Salomon, Gov. Edward (1828–1909)." *Dictionary of Wisconsin History.*

Sayger, Bill. "DeValls Bluff (Prairie County)." *Encyclopedia of Arkansas History & Culture.* http://www.encyclopediaofarkansas.net/encyclopedia/entry-detail.aspx?search=1&entryID=965 (accessed December 13, 2013).

Sesser, David. "Okolona (Clark County)." *Encyclopedia of Arkansas History & Culture.* http://www.encyclopediaofarkansas.net/encyclopedia/entry-detail.aspx?search=1&entryID=7027 (accessed December 13, 2013).

Shea, William L. "The Camden Fortifications." *Arkansas Historical Quarterly* 41 (Winter 1982).

———. *Fields of Blood: The Prairie Grove Campaign.* Chapel Hill: University of North Carolina Press, 2009.

Sherwood, Diane. "Forts of the Civil War." *Arkansas Gazette* magazine section, December 11, 1938.

Schlueter, Herrmann. Herrmann Schlueter Diary, Paul Dolle Civil War Collection, Butler Center for Arkansas Studies, Central Arkansas Library System, Little Rock, Arkansas.

Steiner, Paul E. *Disease in the Civil War: Natural Biological Warfare in 1861–1865.* Springfield, IL: Charles C. Thomas, 1968.

Tenney, Luman Harris. *War Diary of Luman Harris Tenney: 1861–1865.* Cleveland: Evangelical Publishing House, 1914.

Teske, Steven. "Helena-West Helena (Phillips County)." *Encyclopedia of Arkansas History & Culture.* http://www.encyclopediaofarkansas.net/encyclopedia/entry-detail.aspx?search=1&entryID=950 (accessed December 13, 2013).

———. "Rockport (Hot Spring County)." *Encyclopedia of Arkansas History & Culture.* http://www.encyclopediaofarkansas.net/encyclopedia/entry-detail.aspx?search=1&entryID=6171 (accessed December 13, 2013).

———. "Washington (Hempstead County)." *Encyclopedia of Arkansas History & Culture.* http://www.encyclopediaofarkansas.net/encyclopedia/entry-detail.aspx?entryID=5606 (accessed December 13, 2013).

Urwin, Gregory J. W., and Cathy Kunziger Urwin, eds. *History of the 33d Iowa Infantry Volunteer Regiment 1863–6*. Fayetteville: University of Arkansas Press, 1999.

War of the Rebellion: A Compilation of the Official Records of the Union and Confederate Armies. Washington DC: Government Printing Office, 1880–1891.

Official Records of the Union and Confederate Navies in the War of the Rebellion, 30 vols. Washington DC: Government Printing Office, 1894–1922.

Warner, Ezra J. *Generals in Blue: Lives of the Union Commanders*. Baton Rouge: Louisiana State University Press, 1999.

Warren, Steven L. "James Gilpatrick Blunt." *Encyclopedia of Arkansas History & Culture*. http://www.encyclopediaofarkansas.net/encyclopedia/entry-detail.aspx?entryID=5767 (accessed December 13, 2013).

Way, Frederick, Jr. *Way's Packet Directory, 1848–1984: Passenger Steamboats of the Mississippi River System Since the Advent of Photography in Mid-Continent America* (Athens, OH: Ohio University Press, 1994).

Williams, Cindy. "Berryville (Carroll County)." *Encyclopedia of Arkansas History & Culture*. http://www.encyclopediaofarkansas.net/encyclopedia/entry-detail.aspx?search=1&entryID=842 (accessed December 13, 2013).

Wood, Larry. *The Two Civil War Battles of Newtonia*. Charleston, SC: The History Press, 2010.

Worthan, Jacob. "Hollywood (Clark County)." *Encyclopedia of Arkansas History & Culture*. http://www.encyclopediaofarkansas.net/encyclopedia/entry-detail.aspx?search=1&entryID=7159 (accessed December 13, 2013).

The WPA Guide to 1930s Kansas. Lawrence: University Press of Kansas, 1984.

Zbinden, Van. "Memphis and Little Rock Railroad (M&LR)." *Encyclopedia of Arkansas History & Culture*. http://www.encyclopediaofarkansas.net/encyclopedia/entry-detail.aspx?search=1&entryID=2304 (accessed December 13, 2013).

Index

About the Editor

Mark K. Christ is outreach director for the Arkansas Historic Preservation Program at the Department of Arkansas Heritage and has led the agency's battlefield preservation efforts since 1992. Christ is the author or editor of numerous books on Arkansas Civil War history, including *The Die Is Cast: Arkansas Goes to War, 1861*; *Rugged and Sublime: The Civil War in Arkansas*; *"All Cut to Pieces and Gone to Hell": The Civil War, Race Relations, and the Battle of Poison Spring*; and *Civil War Arkansas, 1863: The Battle for a State*. A graduate of the University of Arkansas at Little Rock with a master's degree from the University of Oklahoma, Christ lives in Little Rock with his wife, Kimberly, and daughters Emily and Cassandra.

CPSIA information can be obtained
at www.ICGtesting.com
Printed in the USA
BVHW041650051122
650905BV00002B/97